100 TRUE STORI ... **POWER**

Copyright January 2023
Compiled by Lacei Grabill
Interior Layout and Design: Jamie Walton, Annelise Smith, Michael Malone
Cover design: Jamie Walton

ISBN number: 978-1-939456-40-3

Printed in Michigan

First Printing - December 2022

If this book has changed your outlook on life, strengthened your faith, or deepened your relationship with your Creator, please let us know. Low cost multiple copies are available using the order form at the back of the book or by visiting our ministry website (listed below).

May God bless you as you share the truth with others.

E-mail - truth@searchforthetruth.net
Web - www.searchforthetruth.net
Mail - 3255 Monroe Rd.; Midland, MI 48642
Phone – 989.837.5546

Acknowledgments

A special thanks to ...

My Jesus whose extravagant love for me is beyond anything I could ever understand or deserve. You are worthy of all my praise, and all the glory goes to You.

My forty beautiful friends who agreed to share their personal stories about the greatness of God. Your testimonies have emboldened my faith, and I know they will do the same for many others.

My husband and high-school sweetheart, Keith, who has loved me well for the past 25 years. You never stop believing in me and pushing me to obey God's nudges.

My incredible children and adorable grandchildren who make me feel both blessed and proud on a daily basis. May you have many moments of being wowed by Him.

Bruce Malone, Jamie Walton, Annelise Smith, Michael Malone, and Darla Williams for all your advice, encouragement, and creativity. You believed in this book enough to make it a reality.

Table of Contents BY AUTHOR

Introduction (Don't Skip This!)

What are you "wowed" by? What takes your breath away?

Maybe it's something in nature that stirs that "wow" feeling inside of you: a magnificent snow-capped mountain, a crystal-clear ocean, a raging river ending in a powerful waterfall, the orange-red glow of the sun slipping into the horizon, a delicate flower in full bloom.

Or perhaps it's observing a selfless act that causes you to step back in wonder and amazement: the officer sacrificing his or her life to protect a stranger, the neighbor delivering a meal for a family in need, the child giving his brand-new pair of shoes to a classmate, the radiant bride and groom pledging selfless love to one another, the caring friend who noticed your bad day and showed up with your favorite ice cream. Or maybe the moments you were most wowed by involve your children—their births, first steps, first words, first sloppy kisses. What sweet, precious memories those are for many parents.

Unfortunately, I fall into the category of moms who can't honestly label most of the memories from their children's births as sweet or precious. I also can't honestly say I was "wowed" by most of the experience. Although I may sound like a terrible mother in admitting this, many of the moments surrounding the birth of my first child were more like events out of a poorly-made horror movie. Looking back, I really should have been more prepared. After all, I had heard all the nightmare birthing stories from well-meaning older moms who were simply "trying to prepare me for the big day." Bless their hearts. What an incredible encouragement they were to a nervous first-time mother who was still grieving the loss of her belly button and ability to paint her toenails.

Months before my due date, I had tried my very best to make sure we were ready. (Everything goes smoothly when you have a plan, right?) The nursery was clean, and the crib sheets were on. I had diligently read all the popular pregnancy and child-raising books, and I knew what to expect each month for the next five years. My husband, Keith, and I had taken a labor and delivery class at the hospital, and I was diligently practicing all the proper breathing techniques. I envisioned myself, strong and brave, taking deep, calming breaths as Keith rubbed my back and murmured in my ear about how well I was doing and how beautiful I looked. (Feel free to pause here and laugh at me.)

All of my plans and visions were violently blown up into a million pieces when my water broke two weeks early as I was walking into a church service. I quickly waddled down the aisle to find Keith. I will never forget the look on his face when I told him that we needed to leave for the hospital. His mouth dropped open, his face turned white, and he mustered two words, "Right now?" I nodded, and he literally leapt out of the pew and sprinted to the doors to get the car. At that point I almost lost the father of my baby. In all of his excitement (and downright fear of having to deliver our son himself), he didn't look both ways as he crossed the street, and he was nearly hit by a car.

Thankfully, his life was spared, and Keith met me at the church doors to whisk me off to the hospital. After many hours in my room, the contractions began, and I finally had my glorious opportunity to take those deep, calming breaths—showing the world and my husband what a strong and brave woman I was. (Also, I was looking forward to that back rub.) However, as soon as those muscles started contracting, I discovered my breathing was anything but calm, and I no longer wanted any kind of massage (which was actually a good thing because Keith had almost passed out by this time). The only thing on my mind at that moment was finding an anesthesiologist with some pain meds. I loudly vocalized that desire, was granted an epidural, and was eventually able to get some relief as my body tried its best to birth this stubborn baby boy.

Finally, after 22 hours of labor, including three hours of pushing, the doctor concluded my body was not made for natural birthing, and they prepped me for a C-section. Keith (feeling terrible that I had to go through all of that and still go into surgery) shed some tears for me. What a sweet man. I, on the other hand, was at such a point of mental, physical, and emotional exhaustion that I didn't care how they got the baby out of me. All I knew was I could do no more, and I desperately wanted to see our son. After wheeling me into a surgical room and handing Keith some scrubs to wear, the medical staff went right to work, and we were finally blessed to meet our beautiful baby for the first time.

Although the process of bringing a human being into the world wasn't at all what I had envisioned, expected, or hoped for, the event itself was even more incredible than I could have imagined. I remember the awe and wonder of hearing our son's first cry and then feeling his warm skin as they laid him on my chest. As I put my cheek to his tiny little head and examined his perfectly formed hands and feet, it was as if time stood still. It was entirely surreal. Tears began to flow down my cheeks as the emotions of joy, love, excitement, and relief all mixed together and got stuck in my chest in a way that made my heart feel like it would explode.

In that unforgettable moment I was simply "wowed"—stunned and awestruck at this little life I held.

It seems there is something within all of us longing to be wowed, desiring to experience something that takes our breath away. In this world, there are plenty of things that can help fill that longing. Most likely, I mentioned something earlier that you have been wowed by in your lifetime. But I've intentionally left out the ONE who can wow you more than any other—if given the chance. I've left out the ONE who can awaken you to what it means to truly live, the ONE who desires to speak to you, the ONE who willingly gave His life so you can walk in close relationship with Him. I've left out the ONE whose presence can take your breath away and leave you full of joy and peace in the midst of chaos. That ONE is Jesus Christ. Have you ever been wowed by Him? Have you ever been awestruck at His goodness, His power, His holiness, His love?

I realize this question may be difficult for some of you to answer as you may not know what you think about God or about His existence. Perhaps you do believe in God, but you don't recall an experience with Him that has left you awestruck. A.W. Tozer (a pastor and author from the early 1900's) once said, "What comes into our minds when we think about God is the most important thing about us." Although that may seem like a bold statement, I agree with it because our views about God directly affect how we view ourselves, how we live our lives, and our purpose for living.

Since these are big topics to consider, I'd like to ask you to pause here and honestly consider your answer to this question: What comes into your mind when you think about God? Put a check mark next to each of these statements that you agree with.

» God is good.
» God is the all-powerful Creator of the world.
» God doesn't care about me.
» God speaks to those who listen.
» God deserves my praise and honor.
» God answers prayer.
» God doesn't exist.
» God still does miracles.
» God allows too much suffering to be considered good.
» God desires a relationship with me.

No matter what your experience has been with God, I'm assuming that you put some checkmarks by at least a few of these statements. The purpose of this book is not to debate what you believe to be true about God, His character, or His existence. Actually, the purpose of *Wowed by One* is quite different, and quite less complex. It's designed to share women's stories, their real-life encounters with the God of the universe—their precious moments when they were wowed by Him. Its purpose is to simply bring Him the glory, honor, and praise He deserves.

For some of you, these stories are going to open your eyes to things that you may have heard about but you aren't familiar with. Perhaps you didn't grow up going to church. Or maybe you have gone to church occasionally, but you've never heard stories like the ones in this book, stories of God doing miracles and talking with human beings. I encourage you, actually I plead with you, to open up your mind and heart as you read these stories. You may find there is more to this "God thing" than you ever thought there was.

For others of you, reading these stories may come as a bit of a shock, and you may find yourself a bit confused and uncertain about how to process them. It's easy to believe in the supernatural when we've experienced it ourselves or have seen it with our own eyes. That fits into our preconceived "box" of what God does. It's difficult to believe what we've yet to see. But that doesn't mean it's any less possible or less true. God has never, and will never, fit into any of our "boxes," no matter how hard we try to stuff Him in there. His ways are higher than our ways (Isaiah 55:8), and He is able to do immeasurably more than we can ask or imagine (Ephesians 3:20).

For still others of you, reading these stories will reinforce what you already know—that there is a God, full of power and unconditional love towards you. I would venture to say that this book will cause you to sit in even more awe of Him. You may even (from time to time) feel the need to pause, to place this book on the table beside you, and to take time to praise Him for how incredibly faithful and good He is. You may even be led to read one or more of these stories to your friends or family members to help increase their faith.

My prayer is that this book will cause you to grow in your knowledge of and love for Jesus, no matter if you are still wrestling with whether God is real or you have experienced His goodness and power for fifty years. So, grab a warm cup of coffee or a hot tea, and listen to our stories—His stories. May we never lose our wonder. May we always be wowed by ONE.

" O God, your ways are holy. Is there any god as mighty as you? You are the God of great wonders! You demonstrate your awesome power among the nations."
Psalms 77:13-14 (NLT)

Wowed by THE FAITH OF A PRESCHOOLER
by Karen Hlavin

"Train up a child in the way he should go; even when he is old he will not depart from it." Proverbs 22:6 (ESV)

My husband Jeff and I were very excited that we had the opportunity to go to Florida to visit relatives. Our son Aaron was three years old at the time, and I was seven months pregnant with our second son. We took a couple of days to drive from Michigan to Florida. We were in our twenties and needed to be very careful with our money. Staying in a hotel seemed like such a treat, and we decided that we could save money by bringing a cooler for milk and eating breakfast in our room. At that time, free breakfast wasn't offered in hotels.

We were both big tea drinkers, so I had brought this little heater that would boil a cup of water so that we could have some tea in the room. I put a full, large cup of water into the heater. I thought that Jeff was watching our son, and he thought I was watching him. At the same time, we both looked away, and Aaron grabbed the cup and dumped boiling water all down the front of his blanket sleeper and undershirt. We both saw it happen at the last second, but neither of us were able to get to him in time.

It was that horrific moment when your child is screaming, but at first no sound comes out, and then the face turns pale. Jeff and I were terrified as we unzipped the boiling hot sleeper and removed it and the undershirt. His skin was bright red and had already developed blisters. In some places, the skin was "sagging off" on his chest. It felt like the room was spinning. We both felt panic and terror as we realized that we had no idea where a hospital was. By this time, he was screaming in pain. We quickly grabbed a towel, wrapped it around him and ran to the car.

As Jeff was backing out of the parking space, Aaron managed to say, "Nobody prayed for me!" It was one of those moments when panic had overridden something that we had lived by ever since we had become true followers of Jesus: Go to Jesus first when trouble comes and ask for help. But Aaron had not forgotten what we had taught him. We stopped and took a few seconds to ask Jesus to heal the terrible burns on our sweet little boy. As soon as we were done praying, he stopped crying and said, "There, I'm all better!"

GO TO JESUS FIRST WHEN TROUBLE COMES AND ASK FOR HELP.

We were amazed by the sudden change, and we unfolded the towel to look.

The burn was completely gone. No blisters or sagging skin—nothing was even the least bit red! Aaron didn't seem surprised at all, but I have to admit that Jeff and I were stunned. It was an incredible moment for us as we realized that we had just received a miracle. The faith of a child had led the way.

What an amazing God we have! He is concerned about every aspect of our lives. We have told that story over and over again to friends and family (including grandchildren) through the years. He is there for us if we take time to ask Him in our time of need, sometimes in small ways and sometimes in big ways.

THE FAITH OF A CHILD HAD LED THE WAY.

I have always said that everyone wants to receive a miracle, but no one wants to need a miracle. Miracles are called miracles because they aren't something that happens every day. However, if you ever receive one in your life, you will never forget it as long as you live. We have been followers of Jesus since 1971 (over 48 years), and in that time we have had more prayers answered than we can even remember—and a few of those answers are what I call miracles.

What about you?

If you have children, are you training them to pray for and believe in miracles? Are you teaching them to go to Jesus first when trouble comes and ask for His help?

In Luke 18:17, Jesus says, "Truly, I say to you, whoever does not receive the kingdom of God like a child will not enter it" (ESV). Reflect for a moment on this verse. What do you think Jesus meant by this? How do we receive the kingdom of God like a child?

Wowed by BRILLIANT EYES
by Lynne Biddle

"Are not all the angels ministering spirits sent out [by God] to serve (accompany, protect) those who will inherit salvation? [Of course they are!]" Hebrews 1:14 (AMP)

It was almost 11:00 on a cold, late-October Michigan night. I was driving my 14-year-old daughter home from a friend's house. I looked down to adjust the radio when out of the corner of my eye, I saw something excruciatingly bright and big, and I remember thinking that whatever I was seeing looked like an airplane. It hit our car. The next thing I knew, I was crying out, "Jesus, Jesus!" and I could hear my daughter saying, "Jesus, help us, Jesus!"

Glass was flying in front of my face—seemingly in slow motion. When the minivan I had been driving finally stopped moving, it was laying on its side on the grass, driver-side down. My glance at the radio had caused me to miss the fact that the light at the upcoming intersection had turned to flashing red (as they do every night at exactly 11:00). As a result, we had been T-boned by a pizza-delivery van (not an airplane!) whose driver had been going well over the speed limit.

I COULD HEAR MY DAUGHTER SAYING, "JESUS, HELP US, JESUS!"

After the crash, I was very disoriented. When I realized we had been in an accident, I quickly asked my daughter if she was alright. To my relief, she responded and told me she was okay. However, she was apparently disoriented as well because she quickly unbuckled her seat belt, not realizing she was being held in her seat by it. Since she was sideways and above me, she immediately dropped down and landed on top of me.

Then, before I even had a chance to think of what to do next, we heard a voice from outside. He said, "911 has been called, and they are on the way. Your van is off the road, so you will not be hit again by anyone else. There is no gas leaking, so you do not have to be concerned about a fire. Are you doing alright? Let's see if we can get you two out of there."

Amazingly and miraculously, the sun roof on the van was still operational, so I helped pass my daughter out to this kind stranger, who then pulled me out the same way. Again, it was 11:00 at night, and it was very dark. In that darkness, when I looked at our rescuer, I was taken back by how brilliant and bright blue his eyes were. He told me he had just been out for a walk when the accident happened.

He stayed with us as I called my husband and remained with us until sirens of the police and emergency vehicles could be heard in the distance. Then he looked at me and said, "You are okay, and help is on the way. I have to go now." I thanked him and quickly turned to see the flashing lights approaching, and then I looked back. He was gone—just gone.

I have spent much time pondering the events of that night, and I believe with all my heart that God heard our cries for help and sent an angel. This guardian with the brilliant blue eyes answered every question I could have had before I was even cognizant enough to think to ask them. He had the strength to lift both my daughter and I out of

HE WAS GONE— JUST GONE.

the van, and then he disappeared in the time it took to turn my head. And really, who just goes out for a walk on a dark, ice-cold Michigan night?

What about you?

How does it make you feel when you consider that angels may have been sent on your behalf at some time in your life?

Think of a situation in which God's protection over you was evident, and take time right now to praise Him for it.

"But I cry to you for help, Lord; in the morning my prayer comes before you."
Psalms 88:13 (NIV)

My husband's job was eliminated. This had been the story of our married life. Every four years or so, we would find ourselves in this position. This time was different. Our kids were getting older and established in church, in school, and with friends. We couldn't stay in the same field anymore.

After much prayer, we decided to stay put in our community, and for him to go into a field he had never been in before. This left us with very little income, the start-up expense of our own business, a house, and three small children. We had always had plenty and were able to give when there were needs. Now, however, we needed to learn how to be receivers. It was a humbling and amazing life lesson in understanding both sides of life's moments of transitions. Many people came through for us when we needed it, including our church family.

One of my favorite places to be is in the yard. Our front yard had over-grown bushes all around the house. One day, I decided to pull them all out to keep the foundation clear. After standing back and admiring my day-long work, I realized I had created a bigger problem. I now had multiple holes in my front yard and no money to fill them, let alone get new landscaping.

As I sat day after day on my front porch looking at the big holes, it seemed like this was the last straw. I found myself in lack once again. Yet, this time, I was the cause of it, which, of course, was hard to take. I remember the summer sun beating down on me as I started a conversation with Jesus.

It seemed really selfish to ask for another thing, especially when there were higher priorities like food for the kids and bills to pay. But as I sat in the warmth of the sun, I just started telling Him about the crazy mess I had made, and I explained to Him that I didn't need much, just some dirt. I asked, "Could you, Creator of heaven and earth, get me some dirt?" I needed this one little thing, but it felt like a huge thing. It was a personal thing, a longing, plus its provision would keep the rain out of my basement, which was important too.

A few days later, a man from our church came to my door. He said, "I hear you need some dirt?" I just stared

"COULD YOU, CREATOR OF HEAVEN AND EARTH, GET ME SOME DIRT?"

at him in amazement. I hadn't told anyone about my dilemma or my prayer. Finally, I replied, "Yes, I need all these holes filled." A few days after that, he backed into my driveway with a trailer full of beautiful black dirt. I started filling in the holes with this precious dirt, and my previous conversation with Jesus started filling my mind.

I had really just been venting. I had little faith attached, little hope at all. Yet, I was thankful and repentant. My need was earnest. It was just one of our many times together during that season of lack when I just sat, started a conversation with Him, spoke of my need and left it. I didn't dwell on it or ask others to pray with me. I just had an intimate talk with my Father about a longing, and He heard me. He spoke to someone else to be His hand extended as He lovingly provided, very quickly, the little thing on my heart—dirt.

Each shovelful of dirt going into those holes became a revelation of faith, building up my spirit. I've never forgotten its power, some twenty-five years later.

"I'VE GOT YOU." It's one of the first stories I remember when it comes to faith and provision. If dirt is important to Him, how much more so is healing, provision, and protection? I think of the big dirt pile that was sitting in my driveway as a little wink from the Father saying, "I've got you."

What about you?

Is there a longing of your heart that you haven't yet taken to your Heavenly Father?

If so, start a conversation with Him about it. He cares about even the little things—like dirt.

Wowed by THE FERVENT CHASER
by Jiyoung Kim

"Surely your goodness and unfailing love will pursue me all the days of my life, and I will live in the house of the LORD forever." Psalm 23:6 (NLT)

In this psalm, the psalmist presents two important nouns to us—goodness and unfailing love. In Hebrew, goodness is "tov," which is repeatedly used in Genesis when God created the world. The word for unfailing love is "hesed" in Hebrew, which is hard to describe because the concept is too deep to match the equivalent word in English. It is often translated as "loyal love," "steadfast kindness," or "consistent grace." Also, His unfailing love is based on His solid covenant, so we may say that "hesed" is the covenantal love from the Father God, His love for the people who cherish His promise.

David, who is known as the author of this psalm, maintained that God's goodness and unfailing love would "pursue" him. That causes us to ask this question: "Did David have a secure and perfectly pampered life?" The answer is "no." On the contrary, when he wrote this psalm, he was chased by Saul's army. He was betrayed, harassed, threatened, and persecuted. On top of all of that, he was thoroughly isolated from his family; he was devastated and lonely. From a human point of view, David was a helpless runaway. Nonetheless, in this psalm, David declares that God's goodness and unfailing love would definitely pursue him.

About twenty years ago, I had to use the local "food bank" to feed my two little children while my husband was doing his Ph.D. program. I was new to this country, and I could only speak limited English. Our budget was tight, and we were living off a student visa, so I had no choice. Honestly, it was not easy for me to line up in order to receive some donated food. However, I needed to learn how to lay aside my unnecessary pride for the sake of my family.

I still remember the day I used the food bank for the first time. I waited quite a long time to get bread, eggs, milk, and so forth. Of course, it was a long day for my two little children as well. My little ones fell asleep in my arms. But because I had to carry heavy things, I had to reluctantly wake them up. They barely walked. I felt terrible. To top it off, my hands were slippery because of sweat, and my hands became shaky because of the

I NEEDED TO LEARN HOW TO LAY ASIDE MY UNNECESSARY PRIDE FOR THE SAKE OF MY FAMILY.

weight of the food. So, I accidently dropped one egg carton. Nine precious eggs out of twelve were broken. What a waste! I wanted to save at least three eggs, so I stooped down and picked up the rest of them. People surrounded me and giggled. I was embarrassed, and I blushed.

When my children and I finally got back to the parking lot and loaded the groceries into my trunk, I wanted to jump right in the car and cry. However, at that instant, I saw fresh-cut lavender. The flowers were laid on my front window. I looked around. I did not see anyone. *Who brought the flowers for me?* I smelled the lavender. That sweet scent contained heavenly healing and comfort. I hugged my kids so tight. Oh, there was no better time than that moment to receive this kind of surprising gift—a bunch of lavender. Overcome with emotion, I could not speak but to say, "Father, thank you. I love you." I found myself sobbing, but it was not a bitter cry. It was a good cry of thankfulness for allowing me to see His goodness and unfailing love.

In my entire life, I can confidently say that His goodness and unfailing love have always chased me more rapidly than my bitterness, disappointment, and shame. Twenty years later, by the grace of God, I have become a person who does not have to line up at the food bank any longer. I have learned well how to be a giver through the humble experience of being a receiver. The scent of lavender has still remained in my deepest heart—the unforgettable aroma from heaven. He is the Fervent Chaser. He always runs after me so closely with goodness (tov) and unfailing love (hesed) which is based on His promise.

Thus, just like the psalmist confesses, I say, "Because His goodness and unfailing love will pursue me all the days of my life, I will live in the house of the LORD forever."

What about you?

Are you sometimes harassed by negative feelings or thoughts? Will you describe what they are? Would you be willing to share your honest heart with someone you trust and pray for healing together?

Then, take some time to speak God's truth over you. Believe and confess that God's goodness and unfailing love are chasing you even more closely than those negative feelings.

Wowed by PEACE
by Christina Shafer

"Whether you turn to the right or the left, your ears will hear a voice behind saying, 'This is the way; walk in it.'" Isaiah 30:21 (NIV)

As a college student, I worked with at-risk youth who were court-ordered to live at a facility for a time. We would take them on therapeutic backpacking trips in the woods for eight days. On some of these trips, my role was to move and hide the vehicles away from where we camped. So, I would hide them in places where the teens couldn't see them, but where they were close enough to be accessible if we would have need of them during an emergency.

If anyone knows me, they know I am directionally impaired. I find it quite humorous. I can get turned around in my own town, in which I have lived for over ten years. So, I found this role to be rather daunting, but I felt that God had asked me to do this job, and the place I worked was encouraging me to do it as well. It was incredibly stretching, for it required me to hike by myself through the woods for miles each day.

It was on one of these trips that I came to a literal fork in the trail. I truly had no idea which way to go, and I felt nervous and scared. I remember praying and asking God to show me which way to go. I asked Him to give me His peace, that I would l know the path to take. I remembered Isaiah 30:21, so I prayed and asked God to give me unrest if I began on the wrong trail—that I would know by my lack of peace.

I knew I had a couple miles left to hike before meeting up with the group. As I began to walk, there came a sense of such unrest. With each step I took, the unrest became heavier and heavier. I felt Him calling me back and saying, "Not this way." So, I turned around, and as I began walking the other way, each step became lighter and more peaceful. As I reached the fork and began on the other trail, there was a lightness to my step and complete peace. In a short time, I made it back to the rest of the group.

> **I TRULY HAD NO IDEA WHICH WAY TO GO, AND I FELT NERVOUS AND SCARED.**

God taught me so much through this experience. When I come to a fork in the road or a decision to be made, He often reminds me of this and reassures me that even if I step out on the "wrong trail," He can call me back and redirect my steps—as long as I continue to seek Him. So many times in my life, a lack of peace has been a huge indicator that I am going the wrong way. I hear a voice saying, "Turn around. This is the way." When I don't know which step to take, I remember this, and I ask for His peace and His voice.

I HEAR A VOICE SAYING, "TURN AROUND. THIS IS THE WAY."

What about you?

Do you believe that God can speak into your everyday life?

In what ways has God spoken to you and given you direction?

Wowed by GRACE
by Anonymous

"Let all bitterness and wrath and anger and clamor and slander be put away from you, along with all malice. Be kind to one another, tenderhearted, forgiving one another, as God in Christ forgave you." Ephesians 4:31-32 (ESV)

The Olive Garden is one of my favorite restaurants—soup, salad, and breadsticks. Yum! I have enjoyed every meal there, with one exception. My husband and I were having a date night. We had a great deal to be thankful for: we had beautiful children, friends and family close by, a house to live in, and a great church to be a part of. I thought we had made it, but heading into this date I was feeling anxious.

At the time I wasn't sure why, but now I know it was my womanly intuition. (It's a real thing, ladies!) Shortly after ordering, he pulled out a letter he wrote for me and asked if he could read it aloud. I sat across from my husband and listened to him tell me that for as long as I had known him, loved him, and been married to him, he had been lying to me.

My husband had a pornography addiction, a battle he had been hiding for ten years. Still, even now, writing those words is difficult. In a moment, I felt like my world shattered. I felt hurt, betrayed and unwanted. In the days and months that followed, my mind was bombarded with many haunting questions: *Am I not a good enough wife? How could he betray me so many times? Am I not meeting all his needs? Do I not attract him? Is he thinking of these other women? Is there something about me that he doesn't love anymore? How can he say he loves me but is lying to me? What else is he lying about? Did he ever really love me?*

IN A MOMENT, I FELT LIKE MY WORLD SHATTERED.

There were other times I was just plain angry. At one point, I told a close friend, "I feel like leaving him." One thing is true; he didn't deserve forgiveness. But over time, God changed my heart, so that I could forgive the unforgivable. One of the biggest tools he used to change my heart was prayer. I was led to the book *The Power of a Praying Wife* by Stormie Omartian, and I began reading it. I had to give up a few times because my heart was not ready. I was still dwelling on angry thoughts. I was not willing to forgive. I was not ready to pray for him.

But God didn't give up on me, and that became the tipping point for me to forgive my husband. He didn't deserve forgiveness, but neither did I. Eventually,

I began praying again, and I also began digging into God's Word more than ever before, reading about the way the Lord loves me. I began looking to Him for my worth and identity. Over time, what I discovered was that my heart was softening toward my husband. The grace I received allowed me to give grace out. The more I found my identity as a child of God, the more I forgave him, and the more I forgave him, the more at peace and the more freedom I felt.

We began to focus more on strengthening our marriage, on communicating with each other and spending quality time together. We saw a counselor and confided in close friends for support. My husband had an accountability group he attended, and we installed protection software on all our technology. All those things were beneficial and necessary steps in the healing process, but the process would have taken longer or maybe would have never begun had I not first prayed to God to help prepare my heart for forgiveness.

HE DIDN'T DESERVE FORGIVENESS, BUT NEITHER DID I.

My husband has since told me, "The way you showed grace paved the way for me to experience freedom and healing." Now, thanks to the grace and forgiveness we have both found in the Lord and in each other, our marriage is stronger than ever. There is hope—if you are willing to open your heart to forgive.

What about you?

First, take some time to thank God for the grace and forgiveness He has given to you.

Then, pray that God would reveal to you anyone in your life to whom you need to offer forgiveness.

Wowed by THE BONDAGE BREAKER
by Lacei Grabill

"So you have not received a spirit that makes you fearful slaves. Instead, you received God's Spirit when He adopted you as his own children. Now we call Him, 'Abba, Father.'" Romans 8:15 (NLT)

Ever since I can remember, I have struggled with fear. I remember being terrified of going upstairs alone to put on my pajamas when it was time for bed. I had nightmares often, and I slept with the covers over my head and a row of stuffed animals on each side of my body (to protect me from whatever might come into my room). As I got older, I did ditch the stuffed animals, but I was always afraid that someone was going to try to get into our house.

Then, when I was in 7th grade, one of my worst fears came true. My mom picked me up from school, and we drove to our house in the country. I popped out of the car, ready for an after-school snack, but as I walked into our house, I froze. The frame of the door to our front porch was literally lying on the floor in front of me, and the door itself was hanging slightly open. From where I stood, I could see into the living room and quickly noticed that our stereo and TV appeared to be missing.

As my mom entered behind me and saw the situation, she quickly directed me to go back to the car and lock the doors as she checked the house. I still remember in vivid detail how terrified I was and how slowly time dragged by as I waited for my mom to come back to the car and give me the "all clear." Thankfully, the thieves were long gone, and the police were on their way.

However, although everyone was safe, the thieves were apprehended within a few weeks, and my parents installed a home security system, the experience of the robbery intensified my struggle with fear. As a teenager, I found myself still extremely afraid of being alone, but too embarrassed to admit it. When my parents were gone, I would often walk around my house with my trusty pepper mace can, making sure that I was truly by myself.

My fear followed me into adulthood, and I remember sitting on my bed with my heart racing, quoting Psalms 23 and begging God to help me fall asleep—especially on the nights when my husband had to be gone. I didn't completely understand it then, but I now know that I was living in bondage to fear. I was a slave to it, unable to live any other way. But since I didn't realize it, I simply accepted my captivity, thinking that living afraid was my weakness and my future.

However, one Sunday morning when I was in my thirties, the Lord showed me that living in bondage was not what He had planned for me. The pastor that morning spoke about freedom, and he used handcuffs as an illustration, making the point that God wants to break us free of the things that are holding us back from our true potential.

As he neared the end of the message and invited people to come forward to pray, I knew immediately that I needed to go. But instead of going forward, I began to explain to God all the reasons why a pastor's wife shouldn't respond to an altar call for freedom. *What would people think? Pastors' wives aren't supposed to be in bondage to anything, right? What kind of example would I set for others if they knew that I wasn't living in freedom?*

I then attempted to ignore all the butterflies in my stomach and the lump in my throat. Nothing worked. Finally, I forced myself to follow the leading of the Holy Spirit. I willed my feet to move, trudged down the aisle to the front, and knelt to pray. As I asked Him for freedom, I was overwhelmed by His power and His presence. He took the cuffs of fear I had been wearing for so long and replaced them with His perfect peace.

A decade later, I am ecstatic to say that with God's help, I have not worn those cuffs again. However, in saying that, I want to make it clear that it doesn't mean that I've never had to battle those thoughts again. Every once in a while, the enemy still tries to convince me to live in fear, to walk back into that prison cell. I have to choose to live in freedom. But as I continue to fight and win battles, each time it gets easier, and I know I have an "Abba Father" who is always on my side, fighting with me and for me.

What about you?

The Greek word "abba" actually translates in English as "daddy." Does it feel natural for you to call the Almighty Lord your daddy? Why or why not?

Are you currently in bondage to anything? Allow the Lord to search your heart, and ask Him to show you any area where you might be wearing handcuffs.

Make a list of things from which the Lord has set you free. Then, praise Him for His power and His love.

Wowed by THE SACRIFICIAL LAMB
by Jennie Singer

"'For this reason the Father loves me, because I lay down my life that I may take it up again. No one takes it from me, but I lay it down of my own accord. I have authority to lay it down, and I have authority to take it up again. This charge I have received from my Father.'" John 10:17-18 (ESV)

Jesus became my Savior in fourth grade. However, the significance of that statement did not hit me until about ten years later. I learned a lot about Him during that decade, but I never fully understood the vileness of my sin, His wrath, and His truly undeserved mercy. As I tried and tried to please and serve Him, I couldn't stand up underneath the weight of my sin. It became heavier as high school passed and college began.

I struggled with selfishness, lust, pride, anger, idolatry, and more. It felt like I couldn't get out from under something that was crushing me. This feeling carried into a dream I had one night in college. The dream took place in an open field filled with dried, yellow-brown weeds. I walked through the field and came upon a rectangular pit dug into the ground. As soon as I saw the pit, I noticed myself in it.

The walls came up to my chest, and encircling the rectangle were wooden objects that I understood to be weapons. I felt a dark and evil presence in the pit with me, and I had the sense that I needed to choose one of the weapons, so I did. Immediately after I chose one of the carved pieces of wood, I felt an immense sense of dread and understanding that I was going to die because I deserved to die. The evil in the pit with me was my sin. I knew I couldn't win against it.

The moment I realized that I was going to die, I looked up and saw Jesus and the Father sitting in the field next to the pit. After noticing them, I immediately found myself standing up on the ground next to the pit and in front of Them. I don't remember Their features. I just remember the light that came from Their presence. Though I couldn't see His face, Jesus looked at me and said, "I died so that you don't have to."

Then something happened that scared me for a long time after having this dream: God the Father took a sword and killed Jesus. That was the end of the dream. I woke up crying and afraid. I thought, *How could I dream of such darkness? God did not kill Jesus!* It didn't seem right, and I was confused for several months until I nearly forgot about the dream.

About six months later, the only thing on my mind was improving my grade in my Sustainability in Engineering class. One day, I was meeting with the professor of that class because he was giving me suboptimal grades. (Just kidding. I had earned them!) He was also a Christian, and the topic of our conversation turned to Jesus. My professor told me that if I am a true follower of Jesus, I would be able to answer one question. He said, "What did the centurion see that made him exclaim, 'Surely this man was the Son of God'?"

I left his office with this question and I was determined to find the answer! About a week passed. Eventually, the only thing I could think of were the words of that verse that preceded the centurion's exclamation: "The centurion . . . saw how [Jesus] died" (Mark 15:39). I returned to his office to offer my answer, but it wasn't enough. He asked me to clarify several times. I was ready to give up when the meaning of the dream hit me! I began to sob.

My professor got excited and asked, "What is it? What did you see?" When I could stop crying, I said, "Jesus killed Himself." It sounds odd to say those words, but what I finally understood was that Jesus CHOSE to offer HIMSELF to take the place for MY sin. The Father gave Jesus the authority to lay down and take up His life, and Jesus did just that! The spotless Lamb of God truly died so that I will not experience the death that I deserve.

Today, I praise the Lord for His mercy and for giving me this dream. I thank Him for causing me to cross paths with my college professor, whom He used to drive me to an understanding of Jesus' sacrifice. And I'm blessed with the knowledge of the weight of my sin so I can sing words such as these with confidence:

"For who could dare ascend that mountain, that valleyed hill called Calvary? But for the One I call Good Shepherd, who like a lamb was slain for me." Highlands (Song of Ascent) by Hillsong United

What about you?

How would you answer the professor's question? (What did the centurion see that caused him to believe that Jesus was truly the Son of God?)

At what point in your life did you truly understand the weight of your sin?

Wowed by HIS TRUSTWORTHINESS
by Danielle Spencer

"Those who know your name trust in you, for you, Lord, have never forsaken those who seek you." Psalms 9:10 (NIV)

So often I want to know. I want to know what. I want to know when. I want to know why. However, there are times I don't get to know. I simply get to trust. I get to trust God, the One who does know, who understands fully, who sees everything, who is with me through it all.

My husband and I were excited to be expecting our second child. We made our pregnancy announcement, I got out all of my maternity clothes, and we instantly started looking through our baby name book. However, when we went to our first ultrasound, things were not as we **I SIMPLY GET TO TRUST.** expected. There was no longer a heartbeat for us to hear, and our baby had stopped growing a couple weeks prior. We were shocked. We were heartbroken.

Previously, we had planned a date following our ultrasound to celebrate. I wasn't sure if I still wanted to go on that date. But, my husband thought we should still go, and I am so glad we did. We were able to talk and cry, talk about God's will and about trusting Him, and reach out to our family and friends for prayer. It was one of the best dates we've ever had. God grew us in that moment. He brought us closer to Him and closer to each other as we made Him our focus.

Initially, we weren't sure how to pray. We weren't sure if we should pray for life and a miracle for our baby or if we were supposed to take it as God's will and pray through that. We both ended up feeling that we were supposed to pray for a miracle.

A second ultrasound confirmed what the first had shown. The miracle we had prayed for was not to be, and we were to continue in this season of trusting God when there was no understanding. There were nights following that I felt the ache of not being able to hold our baby. There was an empty feeling from not having our baby in my womb or in my arms. There were days and nights my husband would hold me as I cried, missing the baby we had for such a short time.

I learned in that season that healing can be a process—and that's okay. God was indeed faithful to heal. He gave us a word confirming that someday (in heaven) we will get to hold our baby, and it was like a soothing balm to my aching heart. From that day on, the ache hasn't been there. God brought such a beautiful healing.

He has also made it clear to me that He was there through it all—through the ultrasounds, through the hospital visit, through the ache, through the tears, and through the healing. God met us in such a special way as we turned to Him. I learned to trust God at a whole new level. I was so thankful that I could simply trust Him.

I, most likely, will never understand and will never know why we lost our baby, but I get to choose to trust God. What a gift to be able to turn to God and to trust Him, knowing He will always be there. His unconditional love for us was made so clear, so apparent, so tangible. He is trustworthy, always.

What about you?

Is there something you don't understand right now, and you are having trouble trusting God in the midst of the difficulty? Make the choice today to trust Him, without understanding the "why."

Are you in a process of healing from a past hurt? Give yourself grace, forgive what needs to be forgiven, and keep fixing your eyes on Him.

OUR EVER-PRESENT HELP IN TROUBLE *by Donna Stocker*

"But in my distress I cried out to the LORD; yes, I prayed to my God for his help. He heard me from his sanctuary; my cry to him reached his ears." Psalms 18:6 (NLT)

It was the first day of vacation to visit family. It was a beautiful blue-sky Colorado day. We made arrangements to watch cousins Kevin (a paramedic) and Trina engage in mountain rappelling. They were experienced and led youth groups in this activity.

The entire family (except myself), climbed the 130-foot cliff. As they were making their way up to the top, I sat on a picnic table, enjoying the day and listening to a babbling brook as it sang its song. The chitter-chatter and laughter I could hear from the group began to fade as they ascended higher and higher.

After they made the climb, anchored their gear, and suited up, Kevin and Trina began to descend the cliff. Soon they were both on the ground and on their way back up to do it again (or so I thought). My understanding of this event was that we were watching, not participating. However, once Kevin and Trina reached the top, to my surprise, my youngest son Doug started making his way down the cliff with Kevin.

I tried to suppress my anxiety as none of my boys had ever done this before— much less my baby. So, the self-talk started in. *It doesn't look that hard. His father is up there, and if he's okay with this, I might as well be also. After all, this is what boys do! Besides, Kevin is with him, and he is experienced at rappelling and a paramedic.*

I began to pray. Doug and Kevin came down about a third of the way and rested on a shelf of rock. Kevin asked Doug if he wanted to continue, and Doug gave him the two thumbs up. There were no more resting places after that. The only option was to keep going until boots were on the ground. Almost 30 feet were left to go when all of a sudden, things turned bad. Doug lost his bearings. He could no longer hold the sliding ropes as they were burning his hands. The safety gear malfunctioned, the catch didn't hold, and Doug began to free fall.

I instantly had to choose composure so as to not add hysteria to an already tense situation. My prayer language kicked in, and I was screaming on the inside to God. I witnessed my son falling into a heap, his head just missing a boulder by a sliver. By the positions his legs were in, it was obvious they were broken. As he lay there writhing in pain, it was hard to know how to help him. It wouldn't have been wise to move him, as we had no idea the extent of his injuries. Since we were in the mountains before the time of cell phones, we were off the grid for any way to get help.

Doug's brother ran to the main road until he came to a house. He was able to call 911 for help. The ambulance had to take Doug up the mountain where a helicopter could land and transport him to the hospital. Neither my husband nor I could go with him. As we watched our baby disappear into the sky, it was a long trip down the mountain. When we walked through the doors of the emergency room, we could hear screams. After x-rays and scans, it was determined there were no other injuries except two broken legs. We were told how rare it was for anyone to survive a fall in this kind of circumstance. We had an inner witness that we were walking through a miracle.

Immediately, Doug was taken to surgery. A metal rod was placed from his hip to his knee in one leg. The other leg break was in his growth plate. It would heal naturally, but it would not be weight-bearing for quite some time. His hospital stay was ten days, during which he turned 12 years old. He had a journey ahead of him learning how to walk again. Doug and I remained in Colorado at Grandma's house for several weeks of rehabilitation and physical therapy. Once home, physical therapy continued for several more months. One year later, the rod was surgically removed from his hip. One might ask themselves where was God in all this? I would simply answer by saying this: Doug could have sustained a head or spinal injury causing him to be wheelchair-bound. Doug could have lost his life!

Is it any wonder Doug's schooling led him into the medical arena? Is it any wonder that God's plan and purpose for his life led him to be in hospital administration and management over a rehabilitation hospital in Chicago? Is it any wonder that Doug knows how much God loves him and spared his life? I am so thankful that my screams were heard from heaven, and my cry reached God's ears that day and directed Doug's fall. God saved my son's life and healed his legs completely. I give Him all the glory. "God is our refuge and strength, an ever-present help in trouble." Psalm 46:1 (NIV)

What about you?

Can you think of time-sensitive situations in your life when you needed God's intervention immediately? Take a moment to recall them and express your thankfulness and gratitude to God.

Wowed by PROMISED MASCARA
by Anna McGuire

"Let us hold tightly without wavering to the hope we affirm, for God can be trusted to keep his promise." Hebrews 10:23 (NLT)

When I think back over the span of my life, and the moments when I've been wowed by God, a vivid memory immediately comes to mind. Well, it's actually a series of memories that led to a moment of crying in the parking lot of my favorite makeup store.

When you're a child, everyone asks you on a consistent basis, "What do you want to be when you grow up?" When I was asked this question as a child, I would quickly ramble off something along the lines of "a lawyer" or "a counselor" or "a politician." What's funny is that even from that young age, when I'd share my most basic career aspirations, it was like something (or someone) would gently whisper in my ear, "That's not what you're going to grow up to be." This wasn't a negative voice or a mean rebuke; rather, it felt like an invitation to something that I couldn't have planned for myself.

Early high school years are riddled with even more questions of "What do you want to be when you grow up?" Then come the additional questions about what colleges you're interested in and what you're doing to prepare for a successful adulthood. Although I had the desire to do what God had called me to do, it was much easier to start forging my own plans, instead of waiting on His—until one night when I was confronted by God's plan and promises.

Growing up in the church, I had the opportunity to go to many youth camps and retreats. The summer youth camp before my junior year of high school (the year of high school when you prepare for the dreaded college entry exams and begin to more intentionally seek out college and career options) I was desperate to hear from God about what exactly He wanted me to do with my life. In the front right corner of the camp's auditorium, I pleaded with God to share His plan for me. As I quieted my mind, God quickly spoke to me: "Anna, deep down, you know what I've called you to be. I've called you to be a pastor."

Is it possible to experience shock and lack of shock all at the same time? If so, that's what I was experiencing. Instead of responding back with a "YAY, God!" I gave a quick, "God, ministry is hard—and Bible college can be expensive. How am I going to do this?" He responded to me with a promise that was unlike any other

He had given me before: "Anna, I will provide for you down to your mascara." Yes, that's what He said! The next few moments were filled with thanking God and dreaming with Him about my future.

Fast forward seven and a half years. It was an ordinary Friday evening, and I thought to myself, *I'm almost out of mascara. I need to go to the store to buy some.* I decided to run to my favorite makeup store to pick up it up. Before checking out, I remembered that I had a coupon for a free gift from the store. I was elated to find out at the checkout that the free gift was a tube of mascara! My first thought was *Woo hoo! I don't have to purchase any!* As I exited the store and made my way to the car, God's still small voice said to me, "Anna, do you remember what I promised you?"

Here I am, seven and a half years after that camp moment, a graduate from Bible college, serving in full-time ministry, pursuing my master's degree in counseling, married to my hero, and living in a state that I would've never dreamt of living in—and God hadn't forgotten His promise. He said He would provide for me down to my mascara, and He has done just that, over and over again—a home to live in, a car to drive, finances for college, clothes to wear, food to eat, friends and family to love and be loved by, and even a tube of mascara.

God can be trusted to keep His promises. Even when circumstances seem chaotic or when we lose hope or we don't feel like being faithful to God, He will keep His promises. The seven and a half years between my camp moment and the reminder in the makeup store parking lot were far from easy. Both my family and I faced countless health issues, college was very challenging, and there were seasons where ministry wasn't all that enjoyable; however, through it all, God's promises never stopped. He can be trusted because He's proven himself faithful to His Word in all seasons. God continues to orchestrate my life in such a way that He will keep His promises, no matter what.

What about you?

What is a promise that God has made to you (whether through Scripture or through a conversation you had with Him)?

What areas in your life have you seen God faithful to keep His promises? How can you be encouraged by those to keep trusting God?

REFLECTING HIS BEAUTY

by Melissa Mason

"Don't be concerned about the outward beauty of fancy hairstyles, expensive jewelry, or beautiful clothes. You should clothe yourself instead with the beauty that comes from within, the unfading beauty of a gentle and quiet spirit, which is so precious to God." 1 Peter 3:3-4 (NLT)

This seems like a strange verse for me to quote because I have been in the beauty industry for over thirty-five years. I love the opportunity to help women look and feel beautiful. Yet, although God knows that is important to women, our hearts are even more important to Him. God used a trying time in my life to help teach me that lesson.

In my early thirties, I was very sick and eventually hospitalized several times. I was finally diagnosed with ulcerative colitis (ulcers in the colon). The only treatment that seemed to help was being on steroids. One of the side effects of steroids is weight gain and what is termed moon-face (round puffy face). I really disliked the way I looked. People would comment regularly about my round face or weight gain. Or they would ask if I was pregnant.

I REALLY DISLIKED THE WAY I LOOKED.

This really affected my confidence and self-esteem. One night when I was crying and crying out to the Lord, He reminded me of the verses in 1 Peter and I "happened" on Psalms 34:5: "Those who look to Him are radiant, their faces are never covered with shame" (NIV).

The Holy Spirit touched my heart and helped me to see that my inner beauty was more important than my outer appearance. I knew there was nothing I could do about the side effects of the steroids, so that kind of forced me to focus more on the inside. God helped me realize that I cared a little too much about how I looked and what others thought of me.

In addition, as many of us women do, I was constantly comparing myself to others. Don't get me wrong. I love to do hair and get my hair done. And God knows that women love to feel beautiful. But during that time, God helped me to focus more on the inside beauty. It's a lesson I still carry with me. When I'm feeling a little "fluffy" or don't like what I see in the mirror, I try to remember this: Jesus has made my heart beautiful, and when I look to Him, I am radiant.

What about you?

Do you truly believe that you are beautiful in God's eyes? If that is hard for you to believe, what lies are you believing about yourself?

This week, every time you look in the mirror, speak truth to yourself and say these words: "I am radiant. As I look to Jesus, I reflect His image and His glory!"

Wowed by THE ONE WHO GENTLY LEADS
by Christa Krohn

"He tends his flock like a shepherd: He gathers the lambs in his arms and carries them close to his heart; he gently leads those that have young." Isaiah 40:11 (NIV)

Ever since I have had children, this has been one of my favorite verses. It reminds me that if I learn to lean on the Lord, He will lead me in all my ways as I try to parent them in a godly manner. It reassures me that I can always seek Him for guidance and that He will let me know if I am straying off His path when it comes to raising them right. Little did I know that His gentle leading would start the night before my first child was born.

It was my last day of work. I was thirty-eight weeks into my pregnancy and had been waiting for this day for the last few months. I had two more weeks until my due date and was looking forward to getting a little rest and relaxation before the big day. As I walked into my apartment and turned the corner into the dining room, I saw my husband laying on the floor with his foot propped up on a chair. He had been involved in an accident at work and had injured himself. He came home from the doctor's office later that night in a cast and with crutches.

My dreams of rest and relaxation went out the window! The next three days were spent taking care of him and making sure that he was comfortable. I would like to say that I did all of that with a servant's heart and a gentle and meek spirit, but I would be lying. It makes me cringe when I think of all the griping and complaining that was going on in my head at the time. Others may have not heard it, but the Lord sure did.

Monday night came, and my husband went to my in-law's house to watch Monday night football. Finally, I remember thinking, *some time to myself!* I drew myself a bath, and as I tried to relax, I remember the dialog going on inside my head: *Lord, why did this have to happen? I am so frustrated that instead of David waiting on me, I have to wait on him. Lord, please don't let me go into labor until David is steady on his feet so that he can take care of me. I don't want to do this on my own if he can't help.*

It was quite a pity party—an epic one. Eeyore would have been proud. In the middle of my complaining, the Lord spoke to my heart: "So, you are depending on David to get you through this. What about me?" At that moment, it was like scales fell off of my eyes, and I saw the rotten attitude that I had been nursing for days. I repented and replied to the Lord that I would be relying on Him and that I was placing the timing and the circumstances surrounding the birth of this little one in His hands.

I also decided then that I would submit to His plans and let go of control, even if it meant giving birth with David unable to physically provide all the support I would have liked. Peace washed over me and as I got ready for bed; gratefulness for the Holy Spirit's conviction that brought about a change in my attitude filled my heart.

A little less than two hours later, as my husband and I tried to fall asleep for the night, my water broke. There was no mistaking it. I was in labor. It took me by surprise—but not the Lord. He loved me enough that He made sure that before I went into labor, my heart was right before Him. He worked in my heart to cause me to submit to His will over mine just hours before. In His goodness, He led me there at just the right time.

That next morning, we welcomed our daughter into our family. My husband was wondering why we had a handicapped birthing room. He thought maybe it was because I had a cesarean section delivery. I told him I was sure it had nothing to do with him trying to navigate the room while being in a wheelchair!

> **IN HIS GOODNESS, HE LED ME THERE AT JUST THE RIGHT TIME.**

What about you?

Proverbs 19:21 says, "Many are the plans in a person's heart, but it is the Lord's purpose that prevails" (NIV). Do you find yourself in a season where you are grumbling and complaining to the Lord about the circumstances of life? Do you find yourself wanting to control the outcome of situations instead of trusting in the Lord's process?

Quiet yourself before Him today, and ask the Holy Spirit to show you any areas of your life where you need to "let go and let Him gently lead." He is faithful, and if you are brave enough to ask, He will show you and wash you clean.

"Peace I leave with you; my peace I give you. I do not give to you as the world gives. Do not let your hearts be troubled and do not be afraid." John 14:27 (NIV)

I come from a family of three brothers and no sisters—until I was born. Since I was the baby in the family AND the only girl, I heard stories about my mom being pretty excited about getting her little girl after the three boys! So, I had everything pink imaginable.

One of my mom's and my favorite things to do together was to look at jewelry when we went into the local stores or walked through the mall. (After all, what girl doesn't like her bling?) I remember my mom often saying, "Kristine, if anything happens to me, I want you to have my jewelry, so make sure you get in the house and get all of it." That made me feel a lot of pressure, so I'd always come back with, "Mom, please put that in your will. Please put that it writing." I knew that there were certain pieces that she wanted me to have as an inheritance, but it always bothered me that she didn't promise to get that information in writing.

Well, the day came when my mom unexpectedly passed away, and what an awkward position I found myself in. Who wants to remind their grieving father or brothers what Mom said about her jewelry? Not me! I'm in a pretty good relationship with my sisters-in-law, but I didn't even want to bring up that subject to them.

I vividly remember sitting on my parent's bed, and the four of us (three sisters-in-law and myself) stood around her armoires. They were reaching in and taking things for their daughters (my nieces), which they should have been able to do and I was honestly fine with, I think. But then, my anxiety level began to rise within me to the point I could hardly breathe, and I definitely couldn't speak!

I just wanted to bawl like a baby. My mom had just passed away, and all I could hear in my head was my mom's voice over and over saying, "If anything happens to me, I want you to have my jewelry. If anything happens to me, I want you to have my jewelry." I felt like I was somehow going to be in trouble if I couldn't carry out her wish.

I remember lying on the air mattress in the front room of my parent's house trying to muffle the sobs of my own grief of losing my mom as I heard my dad crying out on the front porch over the loss of his bride of 62 years. *How could I even begin to talk about something so selfish to my dad?* Now was definitely not the time; that was for sure. My brain was so messed up with this grieving thing.

I could hardly contain my sobs when I simply, almost breathlessly, whispered to the Lord, asking Him to help me in my time of grief. It really wasn't about the jewelry. It was about losing my mom. She was, of course, MUCH MORE important than any piece of jewelry, and yet, that was now my only attachment to her. *Was her time on earth really done? Had she really finished the race?*

I remember saying to Him, "Lord, I need your peace, and I need it RIGHT NOW!!" And just like a forceful wind, I had a calmness that was indescribable. I could breathe, I stopped sobbing, and I knew one hundred percent that God was in the room. And then I heard Him say to me, "Kristine, do you know what specific pieces of jewelry your mother really wanted you to have?" "Yes," I answered. Then He asked, "Are they still here?" "Yes Lord, they are," I answered.

MY BRAIN WAS SO MESSED UP WITH THIS GRIEVING THING.

Then I heard Him say, "Then don't worry about any other pieces of jewelry that are already gone. You have just what she wanted you to have."

Again, I don't want you to think that this is all about jewelry. It's about a time in my life when grief was so heavy for me, and the Lord grabbed ahold of my hand when I needed Him the most and blessed me with His indescribable peace!

What about you?

Recall a time when you've experienced God's "indescribable peace" in your life, and then write it down in your journal. Maybe even share it with a friend. This is a testimony of His goodness!

Do you know people who are struggling with anxiety? Take time to pray John 14:27 over them. Maybe even take the time to drop them a note in the mail with this scripture written in it.

"For just as each of us has one body with many members, and these members do not all have the same function, so in Christ we, though many, form one body, and each member belongs to all the others. We have different gifts, according to the grace given to each of us. If your gift is prophesying, then prophesy in accordance with your faith; if it is serving, then serve; if it is teaching, then teach; if it is to encourage, then give encouragement; if it is giving, then give generously; if it is to lead, do it diligently; if it is to show mercy, do it cheerfully." Romans 12:4-8 (NIV)

When I was approached to contribute to this devotional, I had a few initial reactions. First off, I was so incredibly excited and honored to be asked. But, right on the heels of that excitement, before I could even enjoy the happiness, was doubt. I immediately questioned what I would contribute and thought about how my story and testimony wouldn't "stack up" against other women's stories.

I assumed that my feeble devotional would be the worst one and truly wondered why Lacei had asked me at all. I thought of all the incredible, godly, well-spoken women in our congregation and decided that their stories would be better and overall more valuable, with more biblical truth than mine. Now, I realize that was an absolutely terrible way to think and an attack of the enemy, but it was my thought process, nonetheless.

I knew the timeline that Lacei had requested to get the first drafts completed, but I just kept pushing it to the back burner. The more I tried to force my hand and my thoughts onto the page, the more I convinced myself that I had nothing to say of value. Then one day, the Holy Spirit whispered to me: "Why don't you write about the way that you're thinking and feeling?"

I have found that it is very easy to compare our story and gifts to others. I've known many people who are seasoned in their faith and always have the right Bible verse for every situation. And I have many friends who are just prayer warriors through and through. I've thought less of my giftings and story, not because of what these friends have said to me, but simply because I have compared myself to them.

As Theodore Roosevelt said, "Comparison is the thief of joy." I am starting to realize the deep truths

WHY DON'T YOU WRITE ABOUT THE WAY YOU'RE THINKING AND FEELING?

in those words. God never meant for me to compare myself to others. He knit me together in my mother's womb (Psalm 139:13). He knows the plans He has for me, and they are to give me a hope and a future (Jeremiah 29:11). He doesn't want me to look to others and judge myself from that measurement but to look to Him as my guide (2 Corinthians 10:12b). He created me, here on the earth, for such a time as this (Esther 4:14).

COMPARISON IS THE THIEF OF JOY.

There have been times when I've felt like my gifts, what the Lord has done through me and in me, don't measure up to what He's done in others. I am thankful that the Lord reminds me that I am made in His image, for His purposes. I don't ever need to compare my gifts or my story to anyone else's.

What about you?

In what areas of your life does the enemy whisper thoughts of comparison? How do you combat those thoughts?

Why is comparing ourselves with others detrimental to both ourselves and to the church body as a whole?

"For God so loved the world that he gave his one and only Son, that whoever believes in him shall not perish but have eternal life." John 3:16 (NIV)

I gave my heart to the Lord at a neighborhood bible school when I was five years old. My family wasn't a church-going family. If I went to church, my aunt would come and pick my sister and me up and take us to her church. My mom always told us that there was a heaven and a hell. We would pray every night that simple childhood prayer: "Now I lay me down to sleep. I pray the Lord my soul to keep. If I should die before I wake, I pray the Lord my soul to take."

However, by the age of twelve, I wasn't serving God. I didn't go to church much either. But, at the age of fourteen, I met a wonderful sixteen-year-old boy named Don Duford. We went on a blind date with my cousin and Don's friend from their church. I truly believe that God meant for Don and I to meet and fall in love. At the age of fifteen, I asked Jesus to come into my heart and into my life.

I witnessed to my mom and dad as well as my two younger sisters. I would go to church and look around at the pews that were filled with all the other people and their families. I longed for my family to find Jesus and to come and be in church with me.

Over the years, my sisters started coming to church and gave their hearts to the Lord! Then my mom and dad started attending church. My mom gave her heart to the Lord! She is now in heaven waiting for her loved ones to join her. On two different occasions, I went to my precious daddy and asked him if he would like to give his heart to the Lord. Both times, his response was, "I will someday."

My mom passed in February of 2000, and in July of 2000, my dad began to have chest pains during the night. Although he never called his daughters to let us know, the next morning I just felt that my dad needed to be checked on. I called my sister and asked if she could check on Dad on the way to work. As soon as she got to his home, she called me and took him to the emergency room.

I arrived at the hospital on my lunch break and discovered that the hospital had run some tests and were waiting on results. Although I had planned on going back to work, the doctor made it clear that I should stay because of the condition my dad was in.

Then the Holy Spirit prompted me to ask my dad if he was now ready to pray and give his heart to the Lord. I argued. *I couldn't ask my dad that question!* He would think he was about to die. I finally decided to follow His promptings and trust the Holy Spirit. I asked my dad if he wanted to pray and give his heart to the Lord, and he immediately said, "Yes!"

I had the awesome privilege of leading my dad to accept Jesus as his Lord and Savior. Hallelujah! We later discovered that my dad had suffered a heart attack and would have to have open heart surgery. But God brought him through it all. My dad is now 93 years old and still loving God.

In all of this, I've learned to always trust the Lord and be willing to follow the promptings He gives me. His plans are always best, and He never stops pursuing His creation.

What about you?

Do you know where you will spend eternity? If you aren't sure about the answer to this question, please take some time right now to consider making the biggest decision of your life. What you believe about Jesus, and what you do with that belief, determines what happens after your time on earth is over. Jesus claimed to be the Son of God, the King of Kings, the One who came to earth to pay the price for your sins and offer you the incredible gifts of forgiveness, eternal life, and a close relationship with the Almighty God.

If you believe His claims (that He is who He says He is) you must then acknowledge that He is the King and you aren't. That means surrendering control of your life to Him. Although this is easier said than done, in that surrender, you will find freedom, joy, peace beyond measure, and life the way it's meant to be lived. If you don't believe His claims, you must then acknowledge that Jesus was either a liar or a crazy person. He can't be just a "good teacher," because a good teacher would not have consistently claimed to be someone he wasn't, unless He was mentally unstable.

So, what do you believe about Jesus? Has that belief caused you to surrender your life to serve Him? If so, you know EXACTLY where you will spend eternity—in the presence of your Heavenly Father. Romans 10:9 says, "If you declare with your mouth, 'Jesus is Lord,' and believe in your heart that God raised him from the dead, you will be saved." (NIV)

THE ONE WHO HEALS
by Pam Wellington

"But for you who fear my name, the Sun of Righteousness will rise with healing in his wings. And you will go free, leaping with joy like calves let out to pasture."
Malachi 4:2 (NLT)

Through my years as a child of God, I have seen God do many miracles including physical healings. God healed my toddler of a severe pink eye infection one afternoon as I rocked her, praying healing over her. God healed my other daughter's meniscus that she tore while playing high school basketball. As for myself, I was miraculously set free from habitual back troubles not long after receiving Christ as my Savior. One healing story, however, stands out from all the rest because it so drastically changed a young woman's life.

Many years ago, the youth of our church were given the opportunity to lead the Sunday evening service; many of them were leaving on a missions trip the following morning. They did it all—from leading praise and worship to one young person preaching the message to leading in the prayer time at the end of the service. I had gone forward, kneeling for prayer on behalf of a 11-year-old friend of ours named Robert who had recently received a devastating life- threatening diagnosis.

My prayer was that God would heal Robert and spare his life. While on my knees, I could feel a hand on each of my shoulders which meant that two young people were standing slightly behind me, one on either side. As I turned my head to see who was standing to my left, intending to ask him or her to pray, the Lord spoke to my heart, "Not that one, the other one."

So, in obedience, I turned to my right and stood to my feet. I could see that it was a young woman who attended our church, but I didn't know her name. She and I took a few steps away from the altar, and I shared briefly about Robert. We clasped hands as she began to pray for him. Toward the end of her prayer, God again spoke to my heart: "I want you to place your hands on her head like a cap and pray for her."

Really Lord? I don't even know this young lady. She's going to think that's weird or I'm nuts, I silently argued. "Are you going to do it or not?" was His convicting query. I knew God was not messing around. He was looking for my obedience while I was offering up dumb, prideful excuses. I acquiesced and agreed. As she finished up her out-loud prayer for Robert, I asked her name.

She responded, "My name is Tamara." I explained to Tamara that I believed God wanted to do something special for her because He had just instructed me to place my hands on her head like a cap and to pray for her. Much to my surprise, instead of jerking her hands out of mine, she nodded slightly saying she would like that.

I DON'T EVEN KNOW THIS YOUNG LADY.

As I placed my hands on her head, palms down, I suddenly had the worst headache I've ever had in my life. I had experienced this sort of thing previously and knew God was doing this to show me the significant level of pain she was suffering. "Do you have a horrible headache?" I asked. "Yes," she replied without hesitation, "Like most days, I have a very bad headache. I've had acute migraines for most of my life, and there seems to be no medical cure for them."

I realized then that I had heard about this young woman. She was preparing to go on the youth missions trip, but she was forced to lie in the corner during many of the trainings because of the migraines that plagued her.

"Tamara, God has allowed me to feel your headache right now," I stated, "I know He has done this for a reason. I believe His desire is for you to be healed of these migraines—tonight." With my hands still on her head, I prayed out-loud, declaring this healing in her body in the name of Jesus, speaking Bible verses on healing over her. When I opened my eyes at the end, Tamara still had her eyes closed. As I intently watched her face, she slowly began to open her eyes. By the time they were fully open, she was smiling hugely, her face radiant with joy.

"ARE YOU GOING TO DO IT OR NOT?"

Not being able to stay silent any longer, I asked, "Well? How are you feeling?" "It's gone completely!" she declared. We both began hugging each other and laughing. We knew that God had done a miracle for certain! The next morning, the phone rang, and one of my daughters answered. Coming to find me, she said, "Someone is on the phone for you. She says she's Tamara's mom. And she sounds pretty upset."

As I answered the phone, the woman on the other end was crying so hard, she could barely speak. She did manage to say, "Oh, Pam! I just don't know where to begin. Tamara and I are both still in shock. I just had to call and tell you that we are so very grateful to you. You were obedient, and we will never forget this."

She went on to share how horribly her daughter had struggled through the years. Tamara couldn't even walk on concrete sidewalks, choosing instead to walk in the grass alongside them because the tapping of her heels on the cement would bring on an immediate migraine. As she continued talking about other ways these headaches had negatively impacted her child, my heart was filled with even more thankfulness upon hearing all the things God had delivered Tamara from in that one encounter the previous evening.

Tamara did go on that youth missions trip, fully participating in every activity planned. The last I heard, she has never experienced another migraine. She eventually married, and they served as missionaries in the Philippines for several years. The cherry on top of this story is that our young friend Robert (with the alarming diagnosis) is still alive! He's now an adult in his late 30's. I praise God because He actually answered two huge prayers that Sunday night that have reverberated through the years.

SHE NEVER EXPERIENCED ANOTHER MIGRAINE.

What about you?

Have you ever sensed God asking you to do something but didn't want to do it because it seemed "weird"? What happened?

In Galatians 1:10, Paul writes, "For am I now seeking the approval of man, or of God? Or am I trying to please man? If I were still trying to please man, I would not be a servant of Christ" (ESV). Take a moment to pray about whose approval you most often seek.

Wowed by HIS VISITATION
by Janet Yoder

"In the morning, LORD, you hear my voice; in the morning I lay my requests before you and wait expectantly." Psalms 5:3 (NIV)

My husband and I and our children had just moved into a temporary rental house. We were striving to make ends meet, and the deadline loomed for the payment of taxes on our previous home up north that was still unsold. The hard decision was made to sell the beloved snowmobile.

However, the title was nowhere to be found. It was normally kept in the small trunk of the snowmobile, but repeated searches had been futile. We made a trip north to search that house to no avail, then scoured our current home. My husband Homer prayed, "Lord, I don't know where that title is, but you do. If you want us to sell the snowmobile, would you please help us find it?"

The next morning, I asked Homer if he would get some hamburger out of the freezer in the garage. When he came back into the house, he stood in awe as he told me what had happened. He had experienced a strong urge to look, yet again, in the snowmobile trunk. When he lifted the lid, wow! There lay the title in all of its glory—right on top of everything.

Our children were eating breakfast during this exciting news, and my husband asked our oldest son, the primary operator of the snowmobile, where he had found the title. He said, "I didn't find it, but Dad, do you think dogs would know if an angel was near?" He told us that during the night he was awakened by barking, and he looked out the window. Our beagle had been tied near the garage door, and that night he was standing outside, looking into the garage and barking at something. Needless to say, we believe we had a visitation from one of God's ministering servants that night. The snowmobile was quickly sold and the taxes paid—and we marveled at God's timely, spot-on provision.

What about you?

Have you ever asked God to help you find something? Psalms 37:23 says, "The Lord directs the steps of the godly. He delights in every detail of their lives" (NLT). Take some time right now to thank God for this promise.

Wowed by ABUNDANT STRAWBERRIES AND HIS PROVISION *by Wendy Elarton*

"He who did not spare his own Son, but gave him up for us all—how will he not also, along with him, graciously give us all things?" Romans 8:32 (NIV)

I don't think I've ever journaled this story, but the Holy Spirit loves to remind me of it at different times just to make me chuckle. It's a wonderful life lesson about how He is our loving Provider and how much He desires to meet our every need. It's also an example of what happens in those times when we say a quick, short prayer about something without knowing exactly what we are asking for or what we really need.

It was an early morning back at the beginning of church planting. Our days were never the same schedule except for Sunday service at the bingo hall, Wednesday night Bible study at our house, and Thursday youth group. I was knee-deep taking care of my babies and trying to keep up the house. (Our living and dining room became the church foyer, and our upstairs bedroom was the church office). My husband Nathan worked many "Paint by Nate" jobs around the clock to provide for us and the new church.

This particular morning, I was sitting on the stairway looking out the window with one ear listening for my baby, and my heart tuned in as much as I could in prayer. My prayer was something like this: "God, here we are in this neighborhood. You have called us here. Help us reach and care for them." That was all I had the time to say because the fire alarm at the station down the street went off, and men ran out of their houses to answer the call. My baby daughter was awakened too, delighted to start the day and find out what that noise was. My "devoted" time with the Lord was done, and the day began.

As church planters, we had watched God provide sound equipment, an overhead projector, and a screen for our worship. Other churches even gifted us with things that we didn't yet have. On this exceptional day, a pastor invited Nathan to pick up some church nursery things their church had no need for. My husband kissed us goodbye and made his trek up to the Detroit area in his black truck with his "Paint by Nate" sign on the driver's side. Being in charge of children's ministry, I was excited to think we would have a changing table for the bingo hall (even though our nursery was in

GOD, HERE WE ARE IN THIS NEIGHBORHOOD. YOU HAVE CALLED US HERE.

the storage room).

Even after all these years, I can still clearly remember my excited husband coming home after dark with a full truck. Although he would be working the next day, he began to unload his truck. With a big smile, he brought in ten quarts of strawberries through the front door exclaiming, "We have enough strawberries here for us and for our neighbors!" (That was saying a lot because our next-door neighbors had twelve children.) After Nathan came back from delivering the berries next door, we looked at all the ones we still had left, and we decided that our team of volunteers who came for lunch every Sunday would be filled with strawberry shortcake.

As I now reflect back to my prayer on the steps that morning, I think, *Wow, God. You answered my prayer. More than just providing strawberries, You provided our dear neighbors who have been a big part of our church ever since that time.* (Their kids have grown up and have become our youth pastor, office manager, worship leaders, greeters, sound techs, and help to us in many other areas.)

In addition, for the past twenty-four years, we have had many other wonderful neighbors, from all the way down the road to the elementary school to across the street from the church. God not only met our physical need for food, but He also answered our prayer to help build His church by reaching and caring for those in our neighborhood. He hears our prayers, and in His wisdom, "graciously gives us all things."

What about you?

Recall a time when you experienced God's provision. Was it an answer to what you prayed for or a gift that was unexpected?

Take time right now to thank Him for both the big and small things He has provided.

HIS LOVING ARMS
by Linda Chastain

"For we walk by faith, not by sight [living our lives in a manner consistent with our confident belief in God's promises]" 2 Corinthians 5:7 (AMP)

For as long as I can remember, I'd always dreamed of the day that I would become a mother. So, my husband and I decided after two and a half years of marriage that it was time to start a family. We had no idea of the journey we were beginning and how it would test our faith. I was still not pregnant two years later. We walked through the lowest valleys we had ever traveled.

Many of my friends and co-workers were getting pregnant or had recently given birth, and I tried so hard to be happy for each and every one of them. I was in such a vulnerable position for Satan's arrows. *Was I being punished for something? Didn't God love me as much as He loved them? Maybe God knew I would be a terrible mother?* I allowed all of these irrational and faith-destroying thoughts straight from the father of lies to roam freely through my mind.

> **WE HAD NO IDEA OF THE JOURNEY WE WERE BEGINNING AND HOW IT WOULD TEST OUR FAITH.**

Yet, as I dealt with these thoughts, I would then be reminded to focus on Jesus and ask Him to filter my thoughts so I would dwell on the truth of His unfailing love and His lack of condemnation towards His children. I would still sob month after month with the pain and disappointment of "no baby on the way" for that month. But deep in my spirit, I continued to feel like someday I would be a mother.

After two years of not getting pregnant, the doctor said it was time to do some testing which revealed that I had an extremely rare condition which required major surgery on my uterus to even have a fifty percent chance of pregnancy. Surgery to repair this birth defect was a new operation that had just been introduced at a medical conference which my doctor attended. Two years before any of us knew I would need this surgery, God knew and made sure that my doctor attended that conference in which this was discussed.

I felt like this was a sign from God that He was preparing the way for me to finally be a mother! There was a risk factor involved that if I did get pregnant, there was an 80% chance of carrying my baby to full term ending in a C-section and a 20% chance of my repaired uterus rupturing and "bleeding out." If this happened, there was a real possibility of my baby and me dying if we didn't arrive at the hospital in time.

God gave us His peace beyond understanding about our decision to have this surgery. I proceeded with the operation, and not once did I consider the possibility of this journey ending any other way than holding my baby in my arms. My hope was restored. Deep within my soul I heard and knew that God was saying "yes" to our prayers for a child.

About a year after surgery (three and a half years after our journey to become parents began), I became pregnant! We rejoiced and were so thankful to God. I enjoyed every part of being pregnant—even morning sickness. It didn't even bother me that I had to eat saltine crackers in bed before getting up in the morning to go to work (although sleeping in cracker crumbs was not entirely pleasant for me or my husband).

I carried our baby to full term, and she was delivered by C-section. When I saw our daughter for the first time immediately after birth, I just started sobbing tears of joy. She was perfect in every way and of course, the most beautiful baby ever born. We had wanted a baby for so long. The overwhelming love I experienced for her flowed through my entire body, and my heart was captured forever. She was God's promise fulfilled at the end of a long journey.

God's plan and timing are always perfect. I realized later that if my daughter would have come any earlier, I would not have been able to stay home with her as I desired to. No matter how the circumstances appear, keep trusting in God's Word, and keep your eyes on Jesus.

We would have been overwhelmed by depression if the Lord hadn't made His presence known by speaking to us through His Word and saturating us with His unexplainable peace. When our knees buckled, and we sank to our knees in disappointment (almost ready to give up hope), we felt like He physically lifted us and carried us in His loving arms.

What about you?

Has the enemy heaped condemnation on you in the past or even right now? How do you battle it?

Think about a time when Jesus truly lifted you up and carried you in His loving arms. Take time to reflect on that time and thank Him for it.

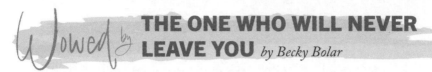

THE ONE WHO WILL NEVER LEAVE YOU
by Becky Bolar

". . . for the Lord your God goes with you; he will never leave you nor forsake you." Deuteronomy 31:6b (NIV)

Being a military wife with small children is a very humbling life, yet one also filled with pride and great sacrifice. It is humbling that I've been able to serve alongside my husband, and I'm proud of the great loyalty with which he serves his country. I've never discounted the sacrifice put forth. There is sacrifice on the part of the service member, the wife, the children, and the entire family—which can dispirit everyone and can grow into a life of loneliness if allowed. However, for my spouse to be successful in his military career, he has to know things are stable on the home front. He has to know his wife can handle the monotony of daily life on her own. He has to trust that I will keep the family life moving and that I will not give up in facing this challenge of military sacrifice.

I remember a day, years ago, when my children were young, I was tidying up my house while they were playing outside. As I went about cleaning, I was in my living room vacuuming when I was overcome with this feeling of loneliness and abandonment. Even worse, I was placing the blame on my husband. I felt so alone! At the time, my husband was stationed at a small Coast Guard search and rescue unit and was working shifts of three days on, three days off, and every other weekend. This schedule was wildly different from my own and that of my kids. All the responsibility that would normally be carried by both mother and father suddenly felt as though I was carrying it all completely alone. It was burdensome, draining, and overwhelming all in the same moment.

The children, as expected, were always in need of care from a mother and father, but I felt I was the only one there. I was the only parent at their side when starting a new school, picking them up and dropping them off, and watching them grow. All the little things like helping with homework, field trips, class parties, sports, dances, and marching band started to add up. I felt sorry for my kids when their father could not be there to sit beside me at his oldest daughter's softball games, to watch his son play soccer, or to cheer for his youngest daughter as she proudly displayed her talent in marching band.

While of course I knew my husband was always there with moral support, I often felt guilt in being the most prominent physical parent in my children's lives. I felt like my husband was missing out on all the little things, like our children growing into wonderful people. These thoughts would creep up over me many times during his thirty-one years of service. There were long stretches of feeling lonely and helpless, feeling left alone to raise the children—left to do life alone. Many times, I questioned if maybe I was not cut out for this life of service and sacrifice.

On this particular day of cleaning, the Lord spoke to me clearly. He said, "You are not alone. I am right here with you. I will never leave you or forsake you. Your husband, your children, and even your friends cannot fill that loneliness the way I can. Lean on Me. I will fill you; I will keep you. I will give you peace when you feel lonely." There is an unmatched feeling of comfort when you know the Father has spoken to you, and there is reprieve when you know He is with you and will not leave you. There is calm in looking to the future and knowing He is there.

At the time, I could not imagine the challenging days that were in front of me, and I'm glad the Lord does not always allow us to see the big picture. There were many challenges in the days, months, and years that would follow; I would have struggled to trust the Lord had I known every adversity that I had yet to face. The days were not always easy, but my faith now would not be as strong had I not faced them. The big picture is for Him to see. He needed me to only trust Him.

With my husband now retired for five years, I am still eternally grateful for that moment of pause and promise from the Lord from many years ago. I am grateful for the care that He showed me in my shadow of weakness. Out of the many hard days, the reward was worth the effort in knowing that the Lord was in my stride and at my side when I needed Him most. It reaffirmed what I always knew—the Lord's promise is binding, and His Word leads us to follow, whether we can see the big picture, whether the sacrifice feels too great, or whether we feel alone or overwhelmed. It is His promise, and we must trust Him.

What about you?

Think about a time when you've felt incredibly alone. What did you do? How did you make it through this difficult time?

Have you ever felt like what you had to sacrifice was too much for you to bear? What happened?

Wowed by THE ONE WHO REMOVES PHOBIAS *by Kelly Newcomb*

"So do not fear, for I am with you; do not be dismayed, for I am your God. I will strengthen you and help you; I will uphold you with my righteous right hand." Isaiah 41:10 (NIV)

In 2011, when my twin girls were in kindergarten, and my son was in second grade, we decided it was time to take the whole family to Disney World, including my parents. I insisted we needed to drive, rather than fly—after all, it would be incredibly expensive to fly seven people to Florida. Plus, I argued, road trips are super fun and build patience and character in kids. My husband refused to drive, pointing out that it would add four days to the time we were gone without any actual enjoyment. The kids would miss more school, he would miss more work, and the list of reasons went on.

Although it's true that I love a good road trip, fear was really the motivator for my vote for driving. I'd always struggled with a fear of flying, since I'd been a teen. I could fly, but I usually had a bout of tears and a fair amount of anxiety before and during. This was the first time I'd ever had to fly with my kids, though, and that was a whole new level of anxiety. When I envisioned flying with my kids, I was gripped with panic. I tried to figure out how I could be with each one of them if the plane went down. I only had two sides for kids to sit on, only had two arms to hold onto three kids. What if we crashed? Who could I grab? Who would be alone?

The closer we got to the trip, the more panicky I became. A couple of weeks before we left, I couldn't even talk about the trip without gulping back sobs as panic choked my throat. I felt terrible. Here my husband was trying to do this wonderful thing and take the whole family on a trip, and my fears were ruining the whole experience. I felt guilty because I knew I wasn't being a good example of faith. Here I was, a Spirit-filled believer, and I couldn't even get ahold of my fears to take a trip. My husband was a doctor, and he suggested Xanax to take the edge off. I agreed to fill the prescription, but it didn't feel right to me. I felt like a terrible witness to my husband and kids. I really felt like God was asking me to trust Him with this.

I had my Bible study group pray for the phobia, and all of my friends were

WHEN I ENVISIONED FLYING WITH MY KIDS, I WAS GRIPPED WITH PANIC.

enlisted to pray as well. Then, two nights before we flew out, a friend announced that she wanted to get a group together to lay hands on me that evening. She gathered some of our friends, maybe five of them, and we sat in my living room after the kids were in bed. I don't remember any specifics, but they all laid hands on me and prayed for the fear to be banished in the name of Jesus, replaced by God's perfect peace.

All the next day, as I finished our final preparations to leave for a week, I listened to hymns and worship music. I had "Tis So Sweet" by Jadon Lavik on replay. I had a playlist of worship songs to play during the flight, a few verses to cling to if I felt fearful, and some gum and motion-sickness medication. I had done all the things I could to be ready. But the big preparation was out of my hands. All day, I had the strangest sensation in my spirit. I felt like something was percolating through my body and soul. It wasn't a jittery sensation, but I felt something stirring all day, almost a bubbling within me.

The next morning, as we headed to the airport, I was AMAZED at the total calm and peace I felt. I had NEVER headed for a flight without some sort of nervousness or fear, and I was usually tearful as flight time approached. This time, I was completely calm and relaxed. I was able to be totally present with my kids as they were so excited to fly and to go to Disney World with their grandparents. I didn't have to infect them with my fear or hide any nerves of my own while I attended to them.

When we landed after the first leg of the trip to Atlanta, I was elated with what I KNEW was God's miraculous deliverance. My husband was perplexed at my sudden tranquility in the face of flying but didn't say much. This was the first time I'd ever seen God do something so undeniably, inexplicably miraculous in my life. With some prayer and some faith, God completely removed my lifelong phobia of flying!

What about you?

Are there certain situations that you know can cause you to have irrational fears?

Take some time to verbalize those fears, and lay them at His feet. Then, rest in His peace that comes from believing that He "will strengthen you and help you."

Wowed by THE ROCK
by Karen Prevost

"O God, you are my God; earnestly I seek you; my soul thirsts for you; my flesh faints for you, as in a dry and weary land where there is no water . . . My soul clings to you; your right hand upholds me." Psalms 63:1,8 (ESV)

Years ago, while we were vacationing in southern Spain, I was strolling along the deserted beach one morning and asked the Lord to speak to me. As I curled up on a boulder jutting out from the sand and watched the tide break against it, I noticed that both snails and barnacles had attached themselves to the massive rock.

Both of these crustaceans were similar in form—soft vulnerable bodies nestled inside a hard protective shell—and they were both holding on to the hard surface. But I noticed a major difference between the two creatures. As the waves crashed against them, many of the snails would lose their grip and be washed away, or I could easily flick them off the rock with my fingers. Yet when I tried to do the same with the barnacles, they tightened their grip even more firmly and would not allow anything to separate them from the rock. Barnacles actually have cement glands that allow them to glue themselves to a hard surface.

Then the Lord spoke to my heart. He is the Rock. He is unmovable, unchangeable, steady, and trustworthy. He is a firm foundation. But, I can choose to be like a snail or like a barnacle. I can casually identify with God, go to church, even read my Bible. However, if He is not the very foundation of my life, when the troublesome waves of life come crashing over me, they will wash me away with the current of the world.

HE IS A FIRM FOUNDATION.

Sometimes, the enemy of my soul will use his tools of deception and condemnation to easily flick me away from the Rock. Or I can intentionally cling to the Rock of my Salvation, making him the center of my life, my reason for being, the One I seek above all other things. I can put my cement glands to work and fill my heart and mind with His truth and spend focused time in His presence. Then, when the storms of life or enemies come to separate me from Jesus, I will only cling more tightly to Him.

The choice lies before us. Will we be like snails, easily detached from our Rock? Or will we be like barnacles, clinging even more firmly to Jesus in the face of difficulty? I choose to be a barnacle.

What about you?

Would you currently describe yourself more like a snail or a barnacle? Which one do you desire to be?

What can you do to be more like a barnacle, clinging firmly to Jesus, the Rock of your Salvation?

Wowed by A SIMPLE PRAYER
by Patty Keppel

"Never be lacking in zeal, but keep your spiritual fervor, serving the Lord."
Romans 12:11 (NIV)

There are times in life when trials and challenges come, and they disrupt the rhythms of what seems to be life's normal. Often, these challenges catch us off-guard like an unexpected visitor, and when this happens, we truly find out how vibrant our spiritual fervor is. Either our fervor will be blown out like a deep breath to a lit candle, or it will be set ablaze like a fire to dry wood, but the defining factor resides in where we keep our focus. This story I will share with you is based on a simple prayer I prayed and how this has kept my spiritual fervor ablaze, as I serve the Lord.

Many years ago, God sent my husband and me four children through the gift of adoption. We first adopted two daughters from birth (who were sixteen months apart), and five years later, we adopted twin boys. These last two little bundles of joy weighed a whopping one pound seven ounces and one pound nine ounces in the neo-natal care unit.

Cody developed normally, while Jared (his twin) did not. When Jared was two-and-a-half pounds in the neo-natal unit, he had a brain hemorrhage that left him somewhat paralyzed on his left side and also gave him a condition called hydrocephalus (too much water on the brain). He required a shunt to be placed in the third ventricle of his brain to drain the excess fluid out. If this fluid is not drained, it can be fatal because the pressure on his brain can build up, resulting in pulmonary arrest. (In other words, he will stop breathing.)

In the past thirty years of his life, he has had this shunt device break down at least nine times which has resulted in brain surgery each time. On one of these occasions, I was alone because my husband Tim was out of town on a day business trip. Jared needed to be seen urgently, so I packed him in the car and took him to see his neurosurgeon. At this point, he was showing major signs of a shunt malfunction. He was listless and semi-conscious with a severe headache and vomiting; he was in very bad shape.

I remember thinking how thankful I was that we were at his doctor's office because we were going to get help. The receptionist soon came over to take us

HE WAS SHOWING MAJOR SIGNS OF A SHUNT MALFUNCTION.

to an exam room, but she quickly informed us that our doctor had fallen off his horse and sustained bad injuries and could not see Jared at all. When she finished telling us this awful news, she left the room for a few minutes to figure out what she could do for us.

At this point, I was holding my son in my arms because of his severe pain, and my heart sunk in despair. I cried out a simple prayer to the Lord: "Jesus, help me to see You in everything." After I prayed this prayer, I begin to look for God's handprint in the events that followed. The next thing I knew, the receptionist returned and had contacted a doctor that Jared had seen in Ann Arbor at U of M hospital. This doctor instructed him to be transferred by ambulance to their emergency room for extensive tests. By this time, my husband had returned home, and he joined me in following the EMS vehicle. We were on our way to what I would soon find out was God's perfect plan of events.

JESUS, HELP ME TO SEE YOU IN EVERYTHING.

Many scans and tests were done on Jared, and the final diagnosis was an infected shunt. The fluid they drew out showed the problem. This was not good. The treatment for this kind of infection generally requires days of antibiotics, but in many cases, the end result is death. It is very hard to get an infection like this under control and eliminated. We knew we needed a miracle, so we prayed and waited out the day.

Often times, while at the hospital, Tim and I will take turns going to the cafeteria to get something to eat and take a break. We never both leave our son's side, so Tim looked up at me and said, "Go and get something to eat." So, I went to the cafeteria and then sat down to pray over my meal.

A woman sitting across the aisle saw me and asked if she could come and join me, and I gladly said yes. The first thing out of her mouth in conversation was, "I can see you love Jesus," and with a smile, I replied, "Yes, I do!" For a glorious hour we shared our testimonies of God's goodness. When we wrapped up our conversation, she asked me if she could come pray with Jared in a few hours when she was done with her shift. Eagerly, I said yes. We gave each other a sister-in-Christ hug and parted.

Two hours later, she showed up at Jared's room and asked if she could pray with him, and again we prayed a prayer of faith together. After a few minutes, she left, and I never saw this woman again. But I knew that she was there to minister a touch of healing in Jared's life. She was God's pick to import His miracle in our circumstance.

The next morning, Jared woke up pretty much back to normal! When the doctor came in to see him, she was very amazed at his vast improvement. They then ran a test to check the fluid to see if it was infected, and the infection was gone! Certainly, the doctor was stumped by his quick recovery. That afternoon, he was released from the hospital, and we knew we had all eye-witnessed a true miracle.

The simple prayer I prayed the day before had ignited my spiritual fervor, and I was able to see God in everything. On so many other occasions I have faced trials, and I have remembered this prayer and what God accomplished.

God wants to turn our trials into triumphs, and keeping our spiritual fervor plays a vital role in that. So, remember the power of a simple prayer, and "keep your spiritual fervor serving the Lord" by keeping your focus on Him through all of life's challenges.

What about you?

When you face interruptions of life's normal, where do you usually direct your focus?

Take a moment to pray a simple prayer that God will help you maintain your spiritual fervor and help you see Him in everything.

OUR FAITHFUL PROVIDER
by Melanie McGuire

"But seek first his kingdom and his righteousness, and all these things will be given to you as well." Matthew 6:33 (NIV)

We had transitioned from a full-time youth pastor position to a full-time lead pastor position. We were living in a parsonage but still trying to sell our previous home. For anyone who does not understand a pay package with a parsonage, it may seem like the pastor has a huge perk because he is living rent-free. Actually though, the salary is lower because of the parsonage. So, we were trying to still pay our other house payment each month with less pay. Our house was on the market, but no one was even looking at it. We prayed, but it seemed like nothing was happening. We couldn't understand why. *If God called us to our new church, why wasn't the other house selling?*

During this time, I remember specifically two instances when God intervened for us. The first was a day at the grocery store, I went with my two children and had just a few dollars to buy some bread and peanut butter. My son began asking for something extra, but I told him that we couldn't get it. Later that very week, someone dropped off one hundred dollars at the church for us to get groceries. We may not always have all of the extras, but God never lets us go hungry.

The other time that God intervened during this season was when a youth intern came. His girlfriend would occasionally come stay with us so that she could see him and help in the youth ministry. One weekend, her parents came to visit and gave us five-hundred dollars for taking care of their daughter to use however we wanted to. That was the monthly house payment for the house we were trying to sell! We were finally able to sell the other house, and we no longer had to struggle each month to make the payment. Praise God that He proves Himself time and time again to be our Faithful Provider.

What about you?

What are you struggling to trust God with today? What Scriptures and promises of God will you stand on?

Wowed by FASTING AND PRAYER
by Traci Presson

"Then no one will notice that you are fasting, except the Father, who knows what you do in private. And your Father, who sees everything, will reward you." Matthew 6:18 (NLT)

April 8, 1995—This day will forever be etched in my mind. It was the day my earthly father met face-to-face with my heavenly Father. It was a long road to that day. You see, four years earlier, my hero (my daddy on earth) was diagnosed with what is commonly referred to as Lou Gehrig's disease—Amyotrophic Lateral Sclerosis. Basically, it is a disease that is completely debilitating physically for the person who has it and absolutely excruciating to the people who have to helplessly watch it happen. The worst part for those with this disease is that their minds are still fully functioning, but their bodies will not cooperate.

As the family member watching, your heart becomes slowly broken. My mom, sister, and I watched as the backbone of our family of four and our spiritual leader became unable to speak, unable to walk, unable to eat, unable to do anything. He had tubes going into his body for nourishment and tubes coming out of his body for waste to exit his system. Even in the later days before he passed, my mom had begun to help blink his eyes so that he wouldn't become blind from the inability to do so himself. Even though this time of life seems like there would be nothing good in it, our heavenly Father was watching over us. Psalm 121:8 tells us, "The Lord keeps watch over you as you come and go, both now and forever" (NLT). He truly was faithful to care for each of our hearts and faithful to walk by our side every day of that season.

AS THE FAMILY MEMBER WATCHING, YOUR HEART BECOMES SLOWLY BROKEN.

My mom and I decided to "fast and pray" for three days to ask for God to either heal our hero or take him on to heaven to be with Him. We agreed together to do this on the fourth, fifth, and sixth day of April 1995. On April 8, 1995, early in the morning, my dad stepped into heaven completely healed and running toward Jesus. I can imagine those first moments between he and Jesus, and they give me an overwhelming peace. Even though the loss on this side of earth was bitterly felt, that picture of the reunion can only make me smile, knowing I will meet my daddy again one day.

I relived that story for two reasons. First, I wanted to remind you of the powerful benefit of fasting along with praying. Matthew 6:18 tells us that God rewards fasting. Fasting tells God that we want more of Him; however, without a spirit of purpose, it's just going hungry. Second, I wanted to remind you of the protection and overwhelming love of God, even when things don't turn out the way we planned.

HE TRULY WAS FAITHFUL TO CARE FOR EACH OF OUR HEARTS AND FAITHFUL TO WALK BY OUR SIDE EVERY DAY OF THAT SEASON.

Open your heart to Jesus today and let Him walk beside you in whatever comes your way. Psalm 91:1 says, "Those who live in the shelter of the Most High will find rest in the shadow of the Almighty" (NLT). Those who go to God Most High for safety will be protected by Him.

What about you?

Take a moment to share with a close friend or family member an answer to a prayer you experienced from a time of prayer and fasting.

If you have never fasted and prayed for a circumstance before today, I encourage you to taste and see that the Lord is good and that He is ready and willing to help you if you will walk in obedience.

Wowed by THE COMFORTER
by BriAnna McGuire

"The LORD is close to the brokenhearted and saves those who are crushed in spirit." Psalms 34:18 (NIV)

This verse speaks volumes whenever we are going through something difficult. God is never going to leave our side. He is beside us. We just have to acknowledge that and repeat it to ourselves so that we can believe it—even if it takes months.

When I was a sophomore in college, the fall semester was rough. I was constantly busy, so I did not make a lot of friends or hang out with the ones I had. I was working, going to classes, helping with a church plant, and trying to make myself do my homework. I also went through a rough breakup during this time, and I was just very lonely.

GOD IS NEVER GOING TO LEAVE OUR SIDE.

After that semester, I did not want to be at school anymore. I just wanted to get away. I felt like the only way for me to get better was to stop focusing on the needs of everyone else and focus on myself. I ended up going home for the spring semester, and I did school online.

That spring was hard. I battled depression, loneliness, anxiety, and a lot of hurt for months. My spirit was tired, and I could barely find any joy. I did not tell anyone how I was feeling during that time because I was trying to be strong and trying to trust in God. I didn't want anyone thinking that I did not trust the plan that God had for me.

I was pushing through, praying and constantly trying to draw closer to Him, but it was like He wasn't speaking. I ended up talking about what I was going through, and when I did, I felt like I could start moving on. Towards the middle of the year, I finally started to feel better. I started to find joy and feel love again.

As I look back on that time, I see how God never left my side. He was constantly making me feel better than I did the day before. I might not have felt complete, and I had really hard days, but I see that God was there, comforting me and showing me His love in multiple ways. I grew closer to my family and saw His love through

I COULD BARELY FIND ANY JOY.

them. I helped in our church's youth group, and I felt His joy through them and their laughter. I went to a retreat and felt His presence in a new way and was able to really open up. I spent alone time with Him and felt His arms wrap around me.

I remember waking up one day and thinking, *I feel God, and I feel joy.* In that moment, I knew that I was finally starting to regain strength and peace. I'm so glad that God never gives up on His children.

What about you?

Have you ever gone through a time when the only explanation of how you made it through was simply God?

Take some time right now and thank Him for bringing you through it. Or if you are going through something now, thank Him for how He will bring you out; declare that over yourself.

Wowed by HIS ABILITY TO SET ME FREE
by Heidi Shearer

"Now the Lord is the Spirit, and where the Spirit of the Lord is, there is freedom." 2 Corinthians 3:17 (NIV)

After college, I decided it was time for me to see a counselor for my eating disorder. I was ready and excited to get well and not keep hurting myself. Yet, as my journey went on with my counselor, I was not getting better. I started having headaches that I had never had before. However, I continued to see this woman and go to a variety of types of therapy techniques. With each technique, I was hopeful I would get better in some way. This woman said that she was a Christian and made many references to Jesus. Due to where this story goes, I don't want to even bring up the ideas that she introduced to me because they create such inner turmoil and try to steal my peace.

After months of therapy, I was transferred to southern California for work. I thought this move was my road to healing! Southern California is known for being a land of healing gurus. I began my search to listen to and learn from many of these popular people in the early 1990's. As I spent money, time, and energy in search of wellness, I became more and more confused. My headaches grew worse, and there was negligible improvement in my eating disorder. I spent months reviewing my childhood and making discoveries about my birth story, and I was able to somewhat cast the blame on these events as to why I was the way I was.

On the journey to get well, I moved to Switzerland in order to start dating the man who would become my husband. While there, I enrolled in a world-class psychology institute in order to pursue a possible career in psychology. This program required me to take classes, study concepts in a group, and to personally take 100 hours of my own psychotherapy. I thought this was my ticket to get well! I was at one of the most elite institutes in the world with people from all over the world. How fortunate was I? Well, maybe not as fortunate as I would have hoped.

My headaches continued so intensely that I was experiencing them every day. The point of this long journey is that I was no more well after two years of this counseling than when I started. Please hear me as I share this; I am not against counseling. This is simply my journey and my outcome. After leaving Switzerland and arriving back to my hometown and family, I was not well. After a very, strong prompting to call a woman that I had met in California, I made the call but didn't know why. Joyce was a very kind older woman who was a pastor's wife and worked at our sales office as the receptionist. When I called her and shared that I was no better than when I left, she said she had a book to send me. Two days later, two books arrived. This was the beginning of being wowed by Jesus.

The books were Victory Over Darkness and Bondage Breaker by Neil Anderson from Freedom in Christ ministries. As I opened the book and saw the chapter titles, my heart started to race with a new anticipation and hope. I asked myself, What is darkness? Is what I have been experiencing considered darkness? That word wouldn't have crossed my mind to describe my circumstances, but that's exactly what I was in—darkness. I wondered what light was and why I hadn't already found it in my pursuit to get well. I discovered it was because I was looking in the wrong places. Jesus Christ and the Word of God (the Bible) became life to me! I had no concept that Jesus was more than my Savior to keep me from going to hell (which I surely didn't want to happen). I had no concept that the Bible was written so that I would know the will of God and how He thinks. As I dove into the books that Joyce sent me, the author took me straight to the face of Jesus, and I saw He was my Savior for my life. I learned 2 Corinthians 3:17, and where freedom truly comes from.

For the days, weeks, and months that followed, I discovered freedom, peace, and joy that I had been longing for and found only when I met with the One. I met Him who loved me, created me, chose me, redeemed me, and now appoints me to go and bear fruit, showing myself to be His disciple. My headaches left me, and my mind was at ease. My eating disorder gradually began disappearing when I learned that I had gone to food instead of Jesus to find my comfort, protection, and peace. I discovered I had allowed food to become a false god to me. It was and still is an incredible journey with Jesus and His Word in the Bible, and this journey continues to lead me and wow me with His ways, peace, righteousness, and joy!

What about you?

Is there anything that you are mistakenly going to for comfort, protection, and peace instead of Jesus? My prayer for you is that you would ask Him to wow you. (He likes to wow us.)

Wowed by HIS PERSISTENT KNOCK IN THE LAND OF BUDDHA *by Connie Steger*

"Here I am! I stand at the door and knock. If anyone hears my voice and opens the door, I will come in and eat with that person, and they with me." Revelation 3:20 (NIV)

I grew up in a large Catholic family, attended a private Catholic school, and even thought of becoming a nun one day. I knew God and the Bible, attended church regularly, and could say the entire mass liturgy by heart, but it wasn't until I found myself living overseas, teaching young people, that I really met Jesus.

I moved to Japan at twenty-four years old when I took a job with the Japanese Ministry of Education to teach English in a public middle and high school. I was placed in a rural location in the heart of the Japanese mountains in a town called Eigenji-cho, which was famous for hosting the largest Za Zen Buddhist Temple in all of Japan. I didn't know anything about Buddhism, and I didn't even speak Japanese before I moved there. But I did enjoy the quiet serene beauty of the mountains, the abundant Japanese maples, and the waterfalls that cascaded throughout my village. It was truly breathtaking.

As I was the only foreigner in a two-hour radius, I was often alone. This was a huge adjustment from growing up in a large family and spending four years serving as a resident hall assistant to help pay for college. I didn't know what to do with my time. It was before the age of internet, and phone calls were reserved for Sunday mornings. There was no TV entertainment. (The BBC English News only came on thirty minutes each day.) So, I took long walks, sat on the temple steps at the edge of the riverbank, and then I started running.

The track coach invited me to join the "Traku Team" at my high school as he had a joy and passion for running. Since he was my vice principal, I thought it wise to accept his invitation. As well, living in the dorms for four years had really packed some pounds on my body, and my physical fitness was in sad shape. I ran a lot, around river beds, down valleys, up steep winding roads, through purple poppy fields, in the village, around the temple steps, across red bridges, over tiny streams, and past the wild monkeys. Running became a real time of reflection, prayer, and thought.

I DIDN'T KNOW WHAT TO DO WITH MY TIME.

Nearly as soon as I started running, I felt a knock on my heart. It wasn't loud, but it was continual—a voice calling me. I didn't know this voice, and I didn't recognize the knock, but it was persistent and ever-present. At this point in my life, I was still searching for my purpose. I had dropped the wanting to be a nun part in college, but I was still wondering why I was born. *What was I supposed to do? Who was I supposed to be?* And then came the knock again—always gentle, always quiet, always present.

One day another English teacher invited me to join the Christian English teacher's group that was meeting on a Sunday afternoon in the city. I was super excited to spend a day with people who spoke my mother tongue as living 24/7 surrounded in a foreign language is truly exhausting for the human brain (until you learn the language). I met some wonderful Christians that day who were nothing like me. They sang really peppy worship songs, they did a Bible study, they prayed out-loud and laid hands on one another, and they welcomed me into their circle with open arms. I remember thinking when I left, *They don't sing my songs, they don't pray like me, they are loud, and not one of them is Catholic.* Yes, this was my first encounter with Protestants, and I loved them!

NEARLY AS SOON AS I STARTED RUNNING, I FELT A KNOCK ON MY HEART.

That Christian support team become some of my closest friends while living in Japan, and my, how my faith grew! However, the knock was still there. It was about a year into my tenure teaching that I attended my first faith-filled weekend, also known as a spiritual retreat. (I went to summer catechism as a child, but it was nothing like this.) We visited a lovely small town a few hours away and spent a weekend at a little Christian resort (not easy to find as less than three percent of Japan is Christian). We sang, we worshipped, we prayed, we heard great messages, we laughed, and we danced.

On the second night, we had a fabulous worship service and then a bit of time before the message would begin. I found a little stone bench in the middle of the rock garden on the edge of a brook. The knock came again. Soon a new friend named Gail (who was one of the speakers at the retreat) walked by and sat by me. She had been in Japan for a few years as a missionary and was also teaching young people. We started talking, and that's when she asked me if I knew Jesus.

Of course, I thought I knew Him. I grew up Catholic; we knew everyone (or so I thought). What I came to know, learn, and understand was that knowing about Jesus and knowing Jesus personally is quite different indeed. Those next thirty minutes with Gail impacted me for the

THE KNOCK CAME AGAIN.

rest of my life. It was in that sweet little spot that I accepted Jesus and prayed the salvation prayer for the very first time.

I knew then it was God knocking on my heart, calling me out—quietly, gently, and never-ceasing. I opened the door and was flooded with the awe, wonder, delight, intimacy, grace, mercy, forgiveness, and incredible love of God. Thank you, Gail. Thank you, Christian friends who reached out to me. Thank you, God—for bringing me to the land of Buddha so I could meet Jesus.

What about you?

Do you truly know Jesus, or do you just know about Him? What's the difference?

If you know Him, spend the next few minutes telling Him all the things you love about Him.

If you think you may just know about Him, are you satisfied with that? God wants to have a living, personal relationship with you, and He will continue to knock until you open the door.

Wowed by UNEXPIRED PRAYERS
by Emily McCarty

"The earnest prayer of a righteous person has great power and produces wonderful results." James 5:16b (NLT)

I was sitting in my bed one night just curiously wondering how many generations would remember me. How long would it be before my stories were forgotten? Please know, this wasn't a sad moment, just a general wondering. A thought raced through my mind, the kind of racing that only happens when God speaks: "Want to be remembered? Pray. Prayers don't expire."

A whole new world opened up before me. Prayers my long-forgotten family line had uttered are impacting my life today. If they hadn't prayed over me, would I know my husband? What about his ancestors? Did they pray for him, his wife, and his children? And then, my thoughts turned to my part in all of this: What kind of impact can I have on my family line? What prayers can I pray for generations after me who may not even know my name?

Prayer is amazing to me. We have unlimited, direct access to the God of the universe. He not only LISTENS to every prayer, but He takes the time to ANSWER every time. Every prayer is important to Him, and He remembers every single one. What a tool He has given us! The all-knowing, all-powerful God is bending His ear to us. We have the power to impact history just by talking, even silently talking!

So keep praying. Pray short prayers and long prayers. Pray long-term prayers and right-now prayers. Pray for your family line and the families of your children's friends. There is no limit to the prayers you can pray and the impact they will have.

My picture may not hang in my family's homes forever; my stories will be forgotten. But my prayers will never stop ringing in the ears of our loving God. He answers them over and over again.

What about you?

What long-term prayers are you praying right now that will be experienced by generations to come? What right-now prayers are you bringing before the God of the universe?

Wowed by THE MIRACLE WORKER
by Kyja Malone

"But let all who take refuge in you rejoice, let them ever sing for joy, and spread your protection over them, that those who love your name may exult in you." Psalms 5:11 (ESV)

You never know when you are just moments away from a miracle. Little did I know, when I woke up on November 6, 2016, that in just a few short hours, I would be a part of a miracle from God.

I was nine months pregnant with our second child and just a few days away from my due date. My husband, Michael, and I were anxiously awaiting this child that we had prayed for and tried for months and months to conceive. We had a beautiful natural delivery with our daughter, so we thought that this second child would have a similar story. There is a saying that goes, "If you want to make God laugh, tell him your plan." Well, I had a birth plan, like many mothers do, and I expected things to go according to my plan.

The night before, I began having contractions but with no consistency, so I just toughed it out. I woke up early Sunday morning and was still having irregular contractions. My husband thought we should go to the hospital, but because I was scheduled to be in the nursery at church and because I consider myself to be a tough person, I was NOT going to call in and cancel working in the nursery just because of a few contractions. (Silly, right? Yes, Michael thought so too.) So, there I was, holding crying babies, changing dirty diapers, and trying to breathe through the pain. Friend after friend came and tried to convince me to head to the hospital. Finally, church ended, and I told Michael, "It's time to go to the hospital!" On our way, my water broke.

Once I arrived, it didn't take long for my "plan" to become derailed. My wonderful midwife broke the news that the baby was breech, and I would have to deliver by C-section. *That wasn't in my plan, God!* Michael comforted me while I cried, and they prepared us to go to the operating room. A few minutes later, I felt something, and it didn't feel right. (Trust me. You don't want the details.) The look on **THAT WASN'T IN MY PLAN, GOD!** the nurses' faces confirmed my fears. This was not normal. Very calmly, the doctor instructed my husband to push the red button on the wall that was behind him.

Immediately, it was like in the movies—nurses came flying into the room, one of them jumped on top of my hospital bed, and they rushed me down the hall to the operating room. Michael stood there shocked, watching them roll his wife away without explanation. Fear began creeping into my heart as I didn't know what was going on or if I was going to wake up to a baby that was dead or alive. The last thing I remember before I "went to sleep" was my midwife praying powerfully in my ear and the nurse saying, "Don't cut yet. She's not out!"

The rest of the story I was told by the medical staff, friends, and family who were there. The strange feeling I experienced was when the umbilical cord fell out (called cord prolapse). This was why the c-section became an emergency. My body, however, was still planning on delivering a baby naturally, so as they were trying to get the baby out, my uterus contracted on his head, and they almost had to cut my uterus to save him. Thankfully, the contraction ended after a minute, but by then he was not breathing. (I'm glad I was out for this part.) They had to do chest compressions to restart his heart before he finally cried that beautiful first cry.

When I woke up after an hour, I finally got to meet our sweet baby boy and hear the most amazing part of the story. Not only had the cord fallen out and caused all this trouble, but they also found it had two true knots in it! Who knows how long those knots had been there. Was it weeks? Was it months? The fact that he was still getting everything he needed to survive through the cord, that he didn't have the cord wrapped around any part of his body when it fell out, and that he was now breathing and crying and cooing—these were all miracles!

We named him Elliot which means "the Lord is my God." In just an hour after leaving church, and during the six minutes after Michael pushed that red emergency button, God had proven that He can do the impossible. Even when things seem out of control, God is watching over each moment of our lives. The Lord reminded me that I can have plans, but HIS plans are better and higher than mine, and they bring Him more glory, which is what life it is all about!

What about you?

Recall a time when God surprised you with His plan which ended up being quite different from yours. How did you respond and why?

What are some ways you can bring Him more glory?

Wowed by THE GOD OF ANSWERED PRAYER
by Kristine Rusch

"In my distress I called to the LORD, and he answered me." Psalms 120:1 (ESV)

The day started off like any other at the Rusch home. My daughter, Kristi, works the night shift, and when she gets home from work in the morning, we sit in our front room and chit-chat over a cup of coffee, and then I leave for work. That's the normal flow of things. However, this particular morning became unusual because after being at work for a little while, I received an urgent call from Kristi.

She was crying so hard that she could hardly catch her breath. Through the tears, she told me that before she went to bed, she had a vision of me mowing the lawn, but for some reason I was lying in the front yard dead, and she couldn't get to me! I reassured her that I was fine, that I was in a meeting with her dad, but I encouraged her to pray about what she saw so that this wouldn't happen.

SHE COULD HARDLY CATCH HER BREATH.

She calmed down and assured me that she would definitely pray before she went to sleep for the day. And my day went on.

Three weeks later, I was out mowing my yard, and I had cut across the road to mow around my mailbox. As I finished mowing, I looked to my right and saw a biker cycling close, so I thought I'd wait for him and then cross the road. What I didn't realize was that as I began to cross, my mailbox blocked my view of a vehicle coming from my left. I walked right out in front of a big, red truck, threw up my left arm, gasped, and said, "I'm sorry" to the driver of the truck. She kept driving, and I kept crossing the road.

I continued working on the diagonal design in my lawn, and then I began to thank the Lord for His protection. The more I prayed, the more I questioned how this red truck had missed me. I again thanked the Lord for His protection and thought, *If she would have hit me, I'd be lying in my front yard!* And then it dawned on me. WOW! This was just the vision Kristi had three weeks ago. I began to thank the Lord that Kristi did take the time to pray for me! I thanked Him for answering her prayer. I thanked Him that I actually suggested that she pray for me. I thanked Him that this lady didn't have to slam on her brakes; the Lord must have told my guardian angel to push me across the road! And I'm so thankful that when Kristi called to Him in her distress, He answered her.

Have you ever had a vision or a dream that you've brushed off as no big deal, and then you realized later that it was from the Lord?

Have you ever been sitting at your desk at work or at home (minding your own business), and you suddenly sense that someone you know is struggling? Or have you ever experienced random pain yourself and somehow known that you should intercede for someone who may be experiencing that same pain?

I challenge you to be willing to be used by the Lord in these ways. He loves to use willing vessels to accomplish His purposes, and He loves to answer prayer.

THE POWER OF PRAYER
by Toni Ellis

"Then he said, 'Don't be afraid, Daniel. Since the first day you began to pray for understanding and to humble yourself before your God, your request has been heard in heaven. I have come in answer to your prayer.'" Daniel 10:12 (NLT)

I have a daughter with autism. She is 31 now. God knit her together in my womb like this and chose her for us, her family. Although three out of every four persons born with autism are boys, God gave me a daughter. Autistic children can be highly intelligent with specific areas of "gifting," like math, or engineering, or music. My daughter has a low IQ, tested by professionals. She functions in decision making and problem solving at about a 10-year-old level. She is socially awkward and frighteningly naïve. When she became old enough to need to start navigating life more on her own, we would plan the day and ask questions about everything in the evening. Always, my biggest concern was just her safety.

She loves to read and is predictable. At the library, she sits in the same spot, on the same floor, at the same time. (Autism equals routine.) This spot (unbeknownst to me) was on the infrequently visited fifth floor of the library. Evidently a man had been watching her. Retrospectively, she admitted he had been occasionally walking by her table saying "Hi" for a few weeks.

One day, he approached her and asked if he could sit down. He eventually offered her a back rub. One thing led to another, and she ended up in a corner, behind a bookcase where he quickly pinned her to the wall and attempted to touch her chest. It finally occurred to her with that physical contact that this "was not good." She shoved him and ran down the stairs, leaving her belongings on the table. She asked for help at the check-out desk. Why did this not turn into something worse? Prayer and God's protection.

Another day she was supposed to be home all day but realized she had left a book at work. We had always driven her to this job. She decided (without calling me) that she would take her bike to get it. She got to work somehow, but on the way home, she got lost. She rode for hours, and didn't answer her cell phone because she thought she'd "get in trouble."

By the time she finally answered her phone, it was dusk, and she had no idea where she was.

> **SHE SHOVED HIM AND RAN DOWN THE STAIRS, LEAVING HER BELONGINGS ON THE TABLE.**

I asked her to look at anything close and tell me what it said or what it was. She said it was all cornfield in every direction she looked. Then, down the road she saw a church. (Does anyone appreciate the irony here?) In the era before smart phones with GPS, I determined her location on the internet with the name of the church. She had ridden south, east, and then north—a total of thirty-five miles trying to find her way home. I picked her up, very sunburned, at sunset. What protected her from this turning into something worse? Prayer and God's protection.

Then, there was the time when we had rented a cabin in a very rural area for a Thanksgiving weekend. She awoke around 5:00 a.m., got a drink, and noticed our smart, trusted German Shepherd sitting right by the door to the outside. He usually did this when we were not staying in our home, but she decided that he must need to go out. Being a dog who did not need a leash, when she opened the door, he meandered out. She waited a minute and then panicked that he was lost.

She wandered out, and found him not far away, but in the darkness did not know which way to go back. She walked the wrong way, despite a bark from the dog, and wandered way off course. The dog followed her the whole way. It was twenty-four degrees, and she had on pajamas and knitted slippers, but no coat, and no shoes. I woke up at around 8:00 a.m. and realized that she and the dog were gone. We had no idea where the next neighbor was or who to call in the county we were in.

I prayed and began looking for who to call while my husband left to drive around. Shortly, a small truck pulled up, and my daughter and our dog got out. A nice lady who lived two miles away had seen her wandering in her back woods area and somehow knew about the rental house down the road. Once again, how did this situation not turn into something far worse? Prayer and God's protection.

What do I know made all these situations turn out okay? PRAYER. I pray for her all the time. When she was young, I worried more. There have literally been so many times over her 31 years when God has had my back; now I just know that I know that I know, God is going to come through.

I don't know what assignments in life God has given you with your children, but God does not give assignments without protection. So, pray for your children. I remember hearing that Billy Graham was asked this question at the end of his life: If he could do one thing over, what would it be? His answer? Pray more.

WHAT DO I KNOW MADE ALL THESE SITUATIONS TURN OUT OKAY?

The passage of Scripture that is my absolute favorite is found in Daniel 10:12-14. An angel comes to Daniel and tells him that his request has been heard in heaven and he has come to answer Daniel's prayer. He then adds, "But for twenty-one days the spirit prince of the kingdom of Persia blocked my way. Then Michael, one of the archangels came to help me, and I left him there with the spirit . . . Now I am here to explain what will happen to your people in the future, for this vision concerns a time yet to come" (NLT).

Apparently, Daniel's answer to his prayer was delayed because the angel bringing it had to fight an evil angel opposing him. Do you know who prayed more than anyone else I know of in the Bible? Daniel. And yet, he had to wait for the answer to his prayer. So much must happen in an unseen world when we pray. I sit and try to imagine it all sometimes. I challenge you to pray, and pray, and pray; it is the absolute best thing a mom can do for her children.

What about you?

Who do you pray for on a daily basis?

What prayer are you currently waiting for an answer to? If you've grown weary in waiting for an answer, encourage yourself with the truth that God sees you, hasn't abandoned or forgotten you, and will answer in His perfect timing according to His will.

Wowed by THE GIVER OF LIFE
by Christina Shafer

"You keep him in perfect peace whose mind is stayed on you, because he trusts in you." Isaiah 26:3 (ESV)

It was five-and-a-half years ago that I gave birth to my daughter, Amariah Grace. Sadly, I was close to half-way through with my pregnancy at the time. It was then He taught me how to truly worship. During the routine check-up, I remember the doctor asking if I had felt the baby move much. I thought to myself, *Of course I have. Haven't I? I mean this is my fourth pregnancy. Surely, I would know if something was wrong.*

But as the appointment continued and an ultrasound was done, I saw my beautiful baby girl. She had died. In that moment a song came into my mind—"Lord, I Need You." I began to sing it quietly as I cried. It was one of the hardest things I have gone through, and yet one of God's biggest blessings as well. It was a journey of healing for me. You see, I had been struggling with a fear of death. I

> **IT WAS THEN HE TAUGHT ME HOW TO TRULY WORSHIP.**

often feared that something would happen to one of my children or my husband. But God showed me what to do in the midst of that—praise Him. This is a journal entry and letter to her and to the Lord that I wrote a couple months after I delivered her:

"How can I miss what I never really saw? How can I miss the sounds of sweet laughter never heard and the sight of freckles unseen? How can I miss words never heard? My heart hurts at times, and yet how can I wish you back? I know one day I'll hear your laughter, see your smile, and hear your voice. One day we will worship side by side.

Lord, you never promised this life would be easy. You never promised I couldn't be hurt or broken, but you did promise to be faithful, to never leave me nor forsake me, to give strength, grace, and comfort. And this you have done. I have experienced your grace firsthand, and it is by your grace I am who I am today.

Those feet, how they are forever ingrained on my heart and my mind—so perfectly formed and so perfectly tiny. Every finger, every toe, every rib was perfectly in place. It has now been months ago that I held you, and then I had to let you go. How I thank God for the pictures, even though they are ingrained in my heart and mind. You are very much part of our family, part of who and what we are, forever loved.

God has used your life to touch so many lives, Amariah Grace, lives I never knew until I had you. You impacted my life, sweet little one. You taught me that in God I am able to do more than I ever thought I could, that every life truly has purpose, no matter how short or how long. When life is given to God, He brings such purpose. I thank God for the gift of you, that I was able to have you even for a short time. I feel honored to have been counted worthy of being entrusted with the gift of you even for a short time.

Your life had meaning; we have been able to pray with or talk about God with so many people because of you. Your life, Amariah Grace, although short, carried purpose and had a heavenly impact.

I simply want to say thank you God for the gift of my sweet Amariah. Please tell her we miss her, and we love her. Praise loud, little one. I'm joining with you from here."

After delivering our daughter, I remember God leading us to have another child. I did not feel ready, but we decided to trust. I got pregnant, and oh, the mixed emotions I felt. The day I found out that we were having a girl was the same day the gravestone was being done, and we had to decide what we

HE BRINGS SUCH PURPOSE.

wanted engraved on it. We also found out that she was due around the time that we delivered our daughter a year ago and potentially could come the same exact day. Through it all, God was there.

There were so many moments of crying out to Him, so many moments of realizing that there truly was no "safe time" for me in pregnancy anymore. I couldn't just reach ten weeks and assume everything was going to be fine. You see, nothing had been wrong with Amariah. They couldn't find one thing wrong and had no idea why she passed. This created anxiety in me, and I worried much of my next pregnancy. Part of me wanted to constantly run to the doctor and get checked to hear her heart. I even thought about buying a heart monitor for my house, but the Lord challenged me on this. He asked me to trust Him. He showed me that He is peace. He reminded me that I can run and get checked and get momentary peace—or choose to simply trust the One who is perfect peace.

He showed me that all the other attempts to find peace only brought momentary relief; it wasn't lasting. I needed to run to the Father, who is peace. Now, we have two daughters. I have a journal with pages filled of how God has used Amariah's life. And I have Katelyn, who brings joy and laughter every day to us and to all who meet her. Again and again, God has reminded me that every day is written. I can trust in His plans and purpose for me and trust that all my days are numbered in His book.

Psalms 139:16 says, "Your eyes saw my unformed body; all the days ordained for me were written in your book before one of them came to be" (NIV). What does it mean to you that all the days ordained for you were written in His book before one of them came to be? Is this an encouragement to you?

Is there anything you struggle to trust God completely with? Are you seeking momentary peace, or the lasting peace of a perfect God?

HIS SNAPSHOTS
by Kelly Rhoads

"I have counsel and sound wisdom; I have insight; I have strength." Proverbs 8:14 (ESV)

As I look back over my life, there are snapshots—pictures in my mind—of the times I truly felt the power and presence of the Holy Spirit guiding, helping, encouraging, and empowering me. So, I am opening the scrapbook of my life and sharing with you my encounters with the Father's goodness:

Snapshot 1: My husband and I were camping, and I was sitting by the campfire. I had been reading a book about the armor of God. As I was looking into the fire, it was as if the presence of God fell on me, and I was engulfed in such love and power, confirming what I had been reading. I was filled with such encouragement of what I had read that I literally felt like I was on holy ground. It lasted about fifteen minutes, and then I felt such peace and calm.

Snapshot 2: I had such a bad hurt, a grievance from someone. I never went to this person as I should have. I bottled up the hurt and shame that accompanied it. I went to counseling, and I read books on forgiveness and how to let it go. After a few months of carrying this weight, I kept praying and asking the Lord to heal this brokenness inside of me. Then, one day I was at a crossroad; I knew I was supposed to pray for this specific person, to pray for this person's good and for me to let go of the pain and to totally release it to the Father. I broke down and truly prayed for this person, for success in Jesus, for this person's life to be victorious. Afterwards, through tears of release, the layers of unforgiveness, shame, and hurt were stripped off of me (off of my mind and heart), and I totally surrendered. I felt so clean, so light and carefree.

Snapshot 3: I was in a season of devouring time with Jesus. I was listening to multiple pastors I respected. I was in the Word and learning to truly worship the Lord. One morning, as I had my praise music on, I started to declare and affirm what the line in the song said, applying it to my life and proclaiming the goodness of God. After hours of this kind of worship, I felt like time just stood still. I felt totally enveloped in the love of the Lord. I felt so in tune with Jesus, like I truly knew what it was like to be in one accord. It was so intimate, so precious and overwhelming. I knew it was a moment of going from glory to glory.

Snapshot 4: I love car rides by myself. It's like my personal sanctuary. One time in particular, I had a three-hour drive ahead of me. I was talking with the Father and I said, "No radio, just a chat with You today." I started praising Him for things He had been so faithful to me about. Then I started telling Him some things on my heart. After a time, I remember saying, "Okay, God. Do You have anything to say to me because this is supposed to be a two-way relationship." As I waited in the quiet, I cleared my mind and focused on Him. I felt a warmth, and then in my mind He gave me three things. It wasn't a long list; it wasn't do this, and this will happen. It was just three things, and I had a knowing of what He meant, and what I was supposed to do with these things. I felt such an understanding of Him in His presence, and I was at complete rest in His care.

I purposely left out the snapshots of Jesus in my life at church. I want to excite you that as you follow Jesus in your life journey, He will always be with you—not just inside the walls of the church. He is the Father who loves and nurtures us better than we can imagine. He is always waiting to have a relationship with us. Yet, it is our choice, to want a relationship with Him. We decide how much we are willing to let go of the things of this world which tie us up. We choose if we will let go of all that holds us back so that we can experience His presence and find joy, peace, and provision in Him. He has given Himself for us at the cross, given us His message and the Word of God, given us many people to preach the good news, and given us beautiful songs of worship. Nothing can match spending time in His Word and presence. He is always beside you, waiting to take that snapshot together. Looking back at my scrapbook, I can truly say, He is worth it all.

What about you?

Are there some things of the world that are tying you up? Will you choose to let them go to experience more of Him?

Thinking back on your own life, what are some snapshot moments with the Lord you would put in your scrapbook?

Wowed by THE ONE I CAST MY CARES UPON
by Amanda Hawkins

"Casting all your care upon Him, for He cares for you." 1 Peter 5:7 (NKJV)

As I look back over my life, I am continually in awe of how God has always met my needs and provided abundantly in every area. I am truly grateful for all the ways He has cared for me, especially in regards to finances. I may not have been so quick to walk in gratitude, however, had I not gone through some difficult times earlier in my life.

As young, newly married adults, my husband and I began to feel the stretch in our finances once our first child arrived. We had made the decision for me to stay at home with our son, and after several months transitioning from two paychecks to one, there were many times that our income didn't quite cover all the expenses each month. We were learning to survive on an extremely tight budget, and saving was definitely not an option. How does one save when every penny is accounted for? I became a master couponer. We traded childcare for favors. We had friends supply us with hand-me-downs. Overall, and with the help of others, we had learned to do everything in our own strength to get by.

But soon an unexpected bill threw a wrench in "our own strength." With this bill, we knew we were going to be short, about one hundred dollars short—which was a lot for us! Worry plagued our hearts and thoughts. We felt like failures. Some of our past choices had put us in this position. Clearly, adulting well was eluding us. Even though we were doing all we could to make the best choices, it still wasn't enough. This bill was more than we had, and by paying it, it would set us up to not be able to pay the next bill, and so on.

The feelings of inadequacy, failure, and shame weighed heavily on our hearts. Reaching our lowest point, my husband and I began to pray. (*Why did we wait until we got there to pray?*) As we prayed fervently for God to provide, God reminded me of a song I had

ADULTING WELL WAS ELUDING US.

learned as a little girl rooted in Scripture: "I cast all my cares upon you. I lay all of my burdens down at your feet. And anytime I don't know what to do, I cast all my cares upon you." It was a difficult pill to swallow, but we resolved to trust God to provide—even when things looked so defeating.

A few days later, I received a hand-addressed letter to me in the mail with no return address. Inside I found another envelope on which the sender had written the simple words, "God told me you could benefit from this." As I opened the inner envelope, I began to weep. Inside was one hundred dollars cash—enough to cover the unexpected bill we'd received just days before! I still don't know who God used to bless us that day, but I hope that by some miracle they are reading this story because I want them to know

GOD TOLD ME YOU COULD BENEFIT FROM THIS.

that their obedience to the Holy Spirit's prompting set in motion a lifestyle of choosing to trust God in every subsequent circumstance.

I can't even count how many times in our now fifteen years of marriage that God has proved His faithfulness by providing our every need. Anytime another circumstance pops up, tempting us to let fear and worry get a foothold, we stop and remember how God came through for us in the past—and how He always will come through! He never fails us, and with each opportunity we've had to trust Him, the easier it has been to trust Him.

That day, we not only received a miracle, but a confirmation of God's promise that He is our ultimate Provider. The envelope we received with those beautifully penned words became a mainstay on my fridge and is still there to this day. It is my constant daily reminder that God has me in His hand and will always supply each and every one of my needs according to His riches and glory.

What about you?

Have you ever waited to pray until you could no longer do it "on your own"? Why do you think you did that?

How do you think God feels when we don't immediately ask Him for help?

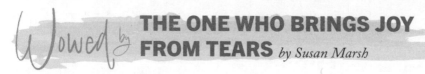

THE ONE WHO BRINGS JOY FROM TEARS
by Susan Marsh

"Those who sow in tears shall reap with shouts of joy!" Psalms 126:5 (ESV)

"Lord, PLEASE don't let me cry as I share Your testimony! I need to be strong!"

Quite a few years ago, I was asked to share at our church's women's retreat. As I prayed about what to share, I sensed the Holy Spirit nudging me to share about the inner healing journey on which the Lord had been taking me during the last year and a half. I wanted to be obedient to His leading, but I knew that in sharing my story in front of forty women whom I knew and loved, I would have to be very vulnerable and expose ungodly decisions that I had made in my past. I feared what others would think of me. Even though the Lord had given me many victories though this journey, I was still raw, still hurting, still in process.

So, I prayed, "Lord, PLEASE don't let them see my tears. Only let them see Your strength in me." And then, with fear and trepidation, I shared about the ungodly decisions I had made in my past, about the healing journey that the Lord was taking me through, and about the transformative love that He was showing me during this time, and then my worst fear came true. When I finished, I sat down

I WAS STILL RAW, STILL HURTING, STILL IN PROCESS.

by the podium and cried buckets of tears—in front of all my friends! I could tell there was a hush throughout the room, and I wanted to crawl under a rock. I felt so exposed, so vulnerable, so hurting, and so concerned that I was not giving God glory by showing my "weakness" in my tears.

And then the most amazing thing happened. I looked up, and there was a line of women waiting to talk with me. Over and over, I heard words of gratitude instead of judgement or condemnation: "Thank you

THANK YOU FOR YOUR TEARS.

for your tears. I thought I was all alone in the pain of my own inner healing." "Thank you for your tears. I always thought you were so perfect and never struggled with any of the things I struggle with." "Thank you for your tears. I needed my heart softened towards women in your similar healing journey."

My heart was filled with gratitude and joy over God's plan of using my tears to impact other women so deeply. Thank you, Lord, that in my perceived weakness of tears, You showed Yourself strong!

What about you?

Are you in a season of feeling raw and "in process" of healing? Have you allowed shame and guilt to isolate you or cause you to feel like you can't be used by Him?

Pray right now for God to provide friends who will encourage you and help keep your eyes fixed on your loving Father. And remind yourself that we are ALL in process.

Wowed by HIS TRUTH
by Kristine Rusch

"We are confident, yes, well pleased rather to be absent from the body and to be present with the Lord." 2 Corinthians 5:8 (NKJV)

On April 18, 2014, I received a call in the middle of the night from my dad. I quickly grabbed my cell phone and made my way to the dining room so as to not wake up my husband Pat. You see, my brother Gary had a bad heart and had been finally placed on the heart transplant list at Cleveland Clinic. I was expecting this call to tell me that Gary was being prepped for surgery to receive his new heart. However, when my dad began to speak, his voice began to break, and I knew that something wasn't right. Although his speech was very broken, he managed to say to me, "It's Gary . . . Gary has just passed away."

Thoughts of shock and disbelief flooded my mind. *What? This can't be right! That is so NOT the news that I was expecting. He wasn't supposed to die; he was supposed to get a new heart!* As I was standing over my dining room table, Pat came out to see what was going on as he could hear me crying. As I finished my conversation with my dad (trying to hold it together), I remember hanging up, and the flood of tears and sobs rolled out of me like a broken dam.

I could hardly breathe. I honestly could hardly catch my breath. Pat and I went back in the bedroom so that I wouldn't wake my daughters, and as I sat on the edge of my bed, all I kept saying to myself out loud was 2 Corinthians 5:8: "To be absent from the body is to be present with the Lord. To be absent from the body is to be present with the Lord. Gary's with the Lord. It's alright. He's with the Lord. It's alright!"

In that moment, I didn't remember where the verse (that I was quoting over and over) was found. Nope, the actual book, chapter, and verse reference never entered my mind. But as a believer, it was hidden in my heart somewhere, and that night that scripture came alive to me! That's what gave me reassuring peace. The **IT'S ALRIGHT. HE'S WITH THE LORD. IT'S ALRIGHT.** truth of God's Word ministered to me like a calming ointment.

Never underestimate the fact that when you're reading the Word of God and you begin to dissect a verse that it's truly being hidden in your heart! At the right time God will bring it to your memory just when you need it. He's faithful at that!

I want to leave you with this. I have awesome memories of my mom, my middle brother Gary, and my dad. I miss them terribly. But I wouldn't want them to "come back" just because I miss them. They're in the presence of the Lord! Imagine that. Being in the presence of the Lord is WAY BETTER than being here on earth.

What about you?

Take just a minute to dissect 2 Corinthians 5:8. If you aren't sure how to do that, let me get you started. The first part of the verse begins with "We are confident." If I look up confident, it means feeling or showing confidence in oneself, being self-assured. Confident is also defined as feeling or showing certainty about something. Then, move on to another word in the verse such as "willing." Look up what it means to be willing. This will be a fun exercise to do, and it will open your eyes to a deeper understanding of the scriptures.

Once you're finished finding the meanings to the different words in 2 Corinthians 5:8, rewrite it to personally apply to you.

If you've experienced the passing of a loved one, know that you're not alone. In those times when the "grief wave" hits you, reach out and grab God's hand. Ask the Lord for His help. He's faithful. Then take time to journal your experience whether it's negative or positive.

Share with others what you're going through. Be honest. It's ok to grieve, but we need each other to help us not "live" there. And remember, you've got this because He is with you through it all.

RESTORATION

by Emily McCarty

"And the God of all grace, who called you to his eternal glory in Christ, after you have suffered a little while, will himself restore you and make you strong, firm, and steadfast." I Peter 5:10 (NIV)

I grew up in the church. I was there every Sunday and Wednesday. Even when my family went on vacation, we would find a church for Sunday morning. We were involved in all different types of ministry. So, imagine my surprise when my parents told us they were getting a divorce. I knew enough about God to not abandon Him, but I was very mad at Him.

The year their divorce was finalized was a hard year full of change. I've never enjoyed change. All my siblings are older, so they began to move away, and my family fell apart. I ended up in a relationship with a nice boy. I put all my trust, time, and effort into him. I was trying to escape my reality. I was still a good Christian girl, but I wasn't giving God much effort. I was giving him my leftovers, if I had any.

Eventually, I slipped into a depression. That darkness was too much for a young relationship, and my boyfriend broke up with me. I was completely alone in a new reality. I was furious with God. Instead of turning to Him, I ignored Him. I didn't trust Him.

Eventually, all of this caught up to me, and I decided life wasn't worth it. I was only sixteen, and I was convinced that my circumstances were too much to handle. I couldn't decide if I wanted to run away or die. I had a packed bag on my right and a bottle of pills on my left.

I WAS FURIOUS WITH GOD.

The next thing I remember is waking up. I had a loft bed that wasn't easy to get into, and I have no memory of climbing into it. God saved my life that night. I wish I could tell you I woke up and everything was fixed, but I still had a long journey of healing ahead of me.

A month or so after that incident, someone told me, "God is faithful to restore." I rolled my eyes, but those words stuck with me. I wasn't sure what restoration would look like. Even though I was unsure and scared, I decided to trust God and let Him handle it. I remember surrendering everything at a youth retreat. I was done being in control of my life. I clearly wasn't very good at it.

Since that day, God has shown up and shown off in my life. He brought me godly friends who challenge me, He has restored my family, and He even gave me the most wonderful love story. My husband and I have two little boys, and my entire family gets together for birthdays and random weekends because we love each other. My **GOD IS FAITHFUL** parents didn't get back together, and I never again **TO RESTORE.** spoke to that boy who broke up with me; God's plan of restoration was different than mine, and I'm so thankful. I am restored.

What about you?

Reflect on a time when things didn't go as you would have scripted them. How did you respond?

What have you learned through seasons of confusion and disappointment?

Wowed by PAIN
by Tammy Screws

"For I am the LORD your God who takes hold of your right hand and says to you, Do not fear; I will help you." Isaiah 41:13 (NIV)

As I walk through my current season of life, this verse has been a gift from God. I just turned forty years old (which is another story), and I just lost my last two baby teeth! As this is not normal, the dentist said something had to be done (either implants or adjustments) to prevent bone density loss or further tooth loss. So, this is my first full day wearing Invisalign. The constant pressure on my teeth is painful. Ouch. The extra saliva is disgusting. Yuck. I had the aligners put on at my orthodontist yesterday, and I didn't even bother taking them out to eat dinner because it felt like too much hassle.

I tried to go for the cheaper option (the aligners that you can do yourself at home), but when they did the simulation showing my end result, it was terrible. So, instead, I decided to pay twice as much at an actual orthodontist to get real Invisalign. The difference is that at the orthodontist's office, they put anchor points on my teeth to grab and help them move; they engage all of the teeth in my mouth to ensure an accurate bite. The orthodontist is not just concerned with the front eight teeth in my smile area, but with my overall dental health. Unlike the at-home aligners, this will not be a quick six-month process while I sleep. Nope, this will be a grueling 18-24 months, day-and-night commitment.

Before I even made the final decision on which option to take, God began speaking to me that these aligners would serve as an analogy for where I'm at in life right now—the Invisalign season. God is not concerned with just the part of my life (my smile) that everyone can see. He wants all of me. There are decisions that I have made recently (choices that are difficult and costly) that may not make sense to many people, other than my safe friends. To most looking in, I may appear foolish, unforgiving, and at fault. That is all they can see. I have learned that I must obey God rather than man. God is doing a deeper and more complete work inside of my heart, engaging my whole self. I would never wish such pain on anyone, and yet I am wowed by my Jesus through this painful season. He has been my Provider, my Protector, my Peace.

I MAY APPEAR FOOLISH, UNFORGIVING, AND AT FAULT.

This is not a quick season of life that I am walking through. Ironically, I had

HE WANTS ALL OF ME.

originally thought that after six months my life would be back to normal (everything would be adjusted and straightened out). But I have been humbled as my former life has been stripped away. I have been left wondering what God is doing. I have felt as though I am treading water some days, and that the next great wave may suck me under at any time. Yet, again and again, I am reminded that God is active and concerned with my overall health—my spiritual, mental, emotional, physical, and relational health. There is no cheaper option or quick fix. Sitting with Jesus daily is what has nudged me in the right direction both day and night.

As I pass through this trial, I have looked back to "anchor" points in my life and have recalled God's faithfulness which has sustained me to know that God is good—ALL the time. My sister was involved in a car accident in high school and sustained a traumatic brain injury; I fell down the stairs when I was five months pregnant and spent time in a wheelchair; I received

I HAVE BEEN LEFT WONDERING WHAT GOD IS DOING.

a call that a close family member was instantly killed; my mother has had cancer. I could go on sharing hard times in my life, times that were not easy, times when I asked why. Still, through it all, God has been my steady. His Word remains true.

In spite of what happens to me, the Truth remains: Jesus loves me so much that He died for me. This world is NOT all there is; our final destination is Heaven. I am thankful I was given the freewill and choice to love and serve Jesus—no matter what may come. I would not have chosen to walk through this current trial. Yet, I would not change the fruit of this season, the character that God is producing in me, or the empathy I have gained for others in their pain.

We all have a choice when pain in life comes; we can run to Jesus or blame Him and run away. I know that when I finally get to take the Invisalign off for good, it will be worth it—my teeth will be healthier and stronger. It will be worth all of the time, money, and pain. In the same way, I trust that there is purpose in the pain of my life; it will all be worth it. My hope is not in having a pain-free life. Rather, I am wowed that even through the pain, Jesus is faithful.

THIS WORLD IS NOT ALL THERE IS.

Give yourself grace. There are times when praying will come easy. There are other times when all you can think to say is "Jesus," and that is enough. Spend some quiet moments now with Him. Speak to Him, even if it's just one word. Sit quietly. Read the Bible and listen. Just keep breathing, and you too will make it through your trial. It will get better. Hold on to hope as you remind yourself of the character of our God.

If you have ever been in a place where you feel as though you don't even have words to say in prayer, then I encourage you to praise. This is how we will overcome! Write down three things that you can praise God for. Even in the most difficult season, God is there. Look around. Look within. Write praises. (It won't make the storm go away, but it may remind you that the sun is still shining above the clouds.)

One way that I have been blessed in this painful season has been through the music of others. Turn on Christian radio or search Christian music on an app or online.

Wowed by HIS CARDINALS
by Karen Hlavin

"Weeping may last through the night, but joy comes with the morning." Psalms 30:5b (NLT)

Years ago, we were getting ready to move from the home in which we raised our kids to a stand-alone condo. I had been praying that our new home would be a place where we would be able to build friendships with our neighbors and perhaps be a positive influence. I remember standing at the kitchen window and saying to my husband, "One of the things I will miss the most about living here is watching the cardinal family that lives in the back yard." Watching the birds brought me so much joy, and they would show up year after year.

On the day we moved into the new condo, I looked out of the kitchen window and the first thing I saw was a beautiful red cardinal in the tree in our backyard. With much excitement, I told my husband that seeing that cardinal was a reassurance that this house was the "home" that God had for us. From that moment on, I knew that we were "just exactly where we were supposed to be."

I told this part of my story to my six-year-old granddaughter on the day she saw a red cardinal in the back yard. She ran and asked me to look at him with her. That year she painted the most beautiful watercolor of a cardinal for me as a Christmas present. I had it framed and hung it in my living room hallway. To this day, it is the most precious thing that I own.

That is the important back story for the real story that I want to share with you. My husband and I had been pastors for many years in a local church setting (which we loved). But after twenty-five years at our church, God called us to serve our fellowship in a leadership capacity, so our responsibility was no longer to the local church but to serve the pastors and churches of our state. Instead of the twenty-five-year celebration that they were planning, it became a good-bye party.

> I KNEW THAT WE WERE "JUST EXACTLY WHERE WE WERE SUPPOSED TO BE."

As anyone in leadership knows, leading isn't always easy, and often you are forced to deal with difficult situations and sometimes people who aren't kind. We found ourselves in one of those very difficult settings one evening at a large gathering. Without going into the details, it was a very painful situation that we were able to get through gracefully.

That night, we had missionaries coming back to our home to spend the night, so I could not process everything with my husband. I did not sleep the entire night. I prayed with many tears and asked God if we had made a mistake by leaving our wonderful church where we felt loved. At this time in our lives, I just didn't want to be in bad situation, and I thought that this could not be His choice for us. I can laugh just a little at that now, but we all have been there.

When morning finally came, I needed to wipe my tears and get up and prepare breakfast for everyone. As I was busy cooking, our missionary friend looked out of the window and said, "Look! You have a cardinal in your back yard." Honestly, I didn't think a lot about it at the time. After breakfast, my husband left for work, and our friends headed home. I was alone, tired, and feeling very sorry for myself as I went into the living room to sit and talk with God.

As I was sitting there, I looked up to see a flock of red (male) cardinals flying from one tree to another all over our back yard! I don't remember exactly how many, but there were probably ten or more of them! It was unbelievable to me. It was as if God was trying to get my attention and show His love and care for me. At that moment, I felt He knew my heart; He felt my pain, and He was with me.

"LOOK! YOU HAVE A CARDINAL IN YOUR BACK YARD."

Of course, I called my husband right away and told him about this miracle that I was watching. He said to me, "Do you remember what your words were when you saw that very first cardinal in our yard? You said, 'I know that we are just where we are supposed to be.'" Then, he asked me, "Honey, what do think God is saying to you right now?"

This was one of the most profound, amazing things that has ever happened to me. These are the moments that have stayed with me, locked away in my heart. My God is such a personal God. He spoke to me in such a personal way that would only be significant to me. When the first cardinal showed up, it didn't register with me at all because I was so absorbed in feeling sorry for myself. So, He spoke even louder!

He spoke to me by reaching to my place of joy as if to say, "Your joy is in Me, not your circumstances. You will always find comfort, contentment, and peace when you look at Me." He reassured me that He heard me and understood my pain. I knew He truly cared and was with us every step. At that moment, God settled any doubts about what He was calling us to do, and at that moment I knew He would give wisdom and the ability to lead well if we continued to seek Him.

I also believe that the Lord inspired my granddaughter to paint that painting.

He knew what it would mean to me. I see it almost every day of my life, and it is the most beautiful reminder of God's love delivered to me through my grand-daughter.

What about you?

Do you know you are "just exactly where you are supposed to be?" Why or why not?

How has God reassured you in a personal way that He sees you, hears you, and understands what you are walking through?

HIS SECURITY
by Debbie Grabill

"God decided in advance to adopt us into his own family by bringing us to himself through Jesus Christ. This is what he wanted to do, and it gave him great pleasure. So we praise God for the glorious grace he has poured out on us who belong to his dear Son. He is so rich in kindness and grace that he purchased our freedom with the blood of his Son and forgave our sins." Ephesians 1:5-7 (NLT)

Even though I've often struggled with the fear of abandonment, God has always been constant. When I was younger, my mother and father abandoned me and did not fight for me. Because of this, I've lived with the fear of being abandoned again. In order to get through this fear, I've often looked at these verses and have been reminded that I am chosen by God and adopted into His family.

Even though I can't depend on my earthly mother and father, I know I can depend on my heavenly Father and on the people that He has put into my life. As I have grown in my faith, calling God my Father has become easier, but it was really hard at first because of the pain I felt from my earthly father.

In my senior year of high school (when I thought I was over this fear of abandonment), all the feelings of my childhood came rushing back. The family that took me in throughout my middle school and high school years had just decided to move out of state, and one of them was already moved. So, at this point, the fear of being abandoned had already started to surface again, but there was one specific moment when the fear exploded.

I was sitting in class when my teacher left the room and told me I was in charge. So when the phone began to ring, I was the one who answered it. As soon as the lady on the other end began speaking, I knew that the call was for me. She said, "Please send Deborah Rodriguez down to the office." Right when I heard these words, my stomach dropped, and I felt sick. This had happened in my childhood many times, and it always meant the same thing. The Department of Human Services was there to ask me a "few questions." So, I hung up the phone, put my things in my locker, and headed to the office with my stomach in a knot.

When I entered the lobby of the office, I was told there was someone waiting for me in another room that wanted to talk to me. As I walked into the room, the man introduced himself, but I didn't really hear what he was saying. For a moment, everything sounded as if I was underwater. As I sat across from him at the desk, the questions that I had heard many times began: "Deborah, do you know the difference between a truth and a lie? If I asked you what color the door was, and it was black, would you say it was red?"

I must have answered the questions sufficiently enough because he began asking me about my family. "Have you been in contact with your family? Do you know where your dad is? Where are your sister's children, and are they safe?" I muttered some answers that I can't entirely recall now, but I do remember saying that I hadn't seen my birth family in years.

But as I left the school and walked to my car, those questions rang in my head over and over again because I didn't know if my sister or dad was safe, or if for some reason I was going to have to leave and go into foster care again. The minute I got to my car and closed the door, I began to sob uncontrollably. It felt like it was happening all over again, that I was being abandoned and couldn't do anything about it.

But God had set everything up perfectly. My boyfriend (now husband) was home from school because of his knee which had randomly acted up that day. Still sobbing uncontrollably, I managed to get to his house where he and his mother consoled me and assured me that I was not alone. They prayed for me, and in a short while, I was feeling much better. I hadn't realized it at the time, but God knew this was going to happen, and he put people in my life who were going to be there for me. I wasn't abandoned by the people in my life, and most of all, I wasn't abandoned by my Heavenly Father.

When we become God's children, we have a Father who is always pursuing us, and even in the darkest moments, He is there. Even in the moments when I've felt the most abandoned, God never left me. I can now thank the Lord who is the Prince of Peace that I no longer have this fear of abandonment. God's love for me is constant and unwavering.

What about you?

Spend some time meditating on the fact that you are chosen by the Almighty God and adopted into His family. How does that make you feel? How does it affect what you believe about yourself and about Him?

How does your past affect your view of God? Is it hard to see Him as a loving Father? Why or why not?

THE ONE WHO HELPS ME DO THE HARD THINGS WELL *by Anonymous*

Wowed by

"And Moses said to the people, 'Fear not, stand firm, and see the salvation of the LORD, which he will work for you today. For the Egyptians whom you see today, you shall never see again. The LORD will fight for you, and you have only to be silent.'" Exodus 14:13-14 (ESV)

In our family, there have been many major announcements throughout the years, but one will forever be etched in my memory. It was the day my son announced that he believed he was gay. A number of emotions coursed through my being—betrayal, failure, and fear (just to name a few). But most of all, I felt determined to pray that my son would not abandon God. I had prayed his whole life that this confusion wouldn't come near him. I remember leaving the room an emotional wreck. I couldn't think. I couldn't talk. I could only cry and ask God, *Why? Why have You betrayed me by not honoring my prayer for my son?*

The days following were long and emotional. I felt numb. I felt I'd been given a hard road to travel. I didn't see it coming. It's not one I would have said "yes" to. I never imagined I would have to travel down this road, but there I was. I asked myself, *What am I going to do with it? Am I going to trust the Lord in it, and let Him lead me, or am I going to give in to the hard road, accept it, and try to fix it myself?*

I admit, in the beginning, I fought it, I cried, I experienced a lot of emotional pain, and I thought my heart would break. But, after my initial child-like tantrum, the Holy Spirit reminded me of my own thoughts a few years back: *If I have to face a hard task, I want to do it well, showing that Jesus is right there with me. I want to walk through it knowing that He sees me, and I want others to see Jesus in me.*

The Lord knows my hurt and my heart ache; He sees me, and He's in this storm with me. Being battle weary is a real thing. The feelings are real, the questioning in the waiting is real, the why's are real, the wanting to give up in the middle or right before the miracle is also real. It's hard to say, "Your will be done in my children's lives." There's a huge unknown when we pray this way, but we also know His will and His ways are better than our ways.

I only have to remember the faithfulness of God, all the times He has come through with an answered prayer at just the right time. I only have to remember the things He's done to keep us and sustain us in the storm. I only have to continue to trust Him in the storm and be led by the Holy Spirit. He is my hope, the One who moves mountains. He is the One who is fighting for me, the One in the battle with me. I don't have to fight any battle on my own.

It has been 1,075 days since my son's announcement. I've prayed for him every single one of those days, and I will continue to pray for the Lord to surround him with His love and to speak life into him. The Lord hasn't betrayed us, hasn't left us, and hasn't stopped loving us. God hasn't left us to do this alone. He is and will always be right beside us, giving us the strength to do this hard thing well.

GOD HASN'T LEFT US TO DO THIS ALONE.

What about you?

Do you find yourself on a road that you never thought you would have to travel down?

How are you responding to it? With faith? Fear? Anger? Confusion?

Ask the Lord to give you the strength to do this hard thing well, and then trust that He is right there with you, fighting for you.

Wowed by THE ONE WHO SUPPLIES
by Janet Yoder

"So do not worry, saying, 'What shall we eat?' or 'What shall we drink?' Or 'What shall we wear?'" Matthew 6:31 (NIV)

My husband, Homer, and I along with our four children were about to enter a new phase of our lives. We had completed five years of working in a home for boys who had been sent to us by the probate court. Although we loved the work and the boys as well, my husband became increasingly aware that God was calling him to the ministry of pastoring. After much soul searching and prayer, seeking the will of God and guidance, the decision was made to press forward. We eventually received and accepted an invitation from a church in Three Rivers, Michigan.

A three-month period spanned the ending of our work at the boy's home and the beginning of our time serving the Moorepark Church—three months without pay. We learned to live frugally, but eventually the cupboard's food supply dwindled dramatically. I recall telling my husband that if we could just afford to get some of the basics like sugar, flour, and eggs, we would be alright for a while.

We prayed for our daily bread. Within several days, Homer's parents came for a visit from out-of-state, bringing a goodie bag with them which included flour and sugar. The eggs came as a providential blessing from God in a most unusual way—which deepened our love for Him and caused us to trust in His ingenious wisdom.

New neighbors from a large metropolis moved into a heavily wooded area near our home with the intentions of farming. We snickered at their naïve hopes (for certainly their property was not "farm potential"). One day, the new neighbor knocked on our door and asked Homer if he would come with him to look at his cattle. He thought a mountain lion may have attacked them because they had bite marks on their flanks.

WE PRAYED FOR OUR DAILY BREAD.

After inspecting the cattle and looking around, Homer said, "I think the real culprits may be those two German Shepherds over there." And so, the guilty pair was found out. The next day there was another knock at our door, and behold, our good neighbor stood there, holding two dozen fresh eggs! God is so good. He not only provides for our needs, but with His rich sense of humor, he knew how to teach His smug children the lesson of humility as well as gratefulness.

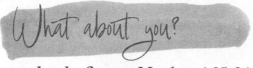

Take some time to read and reflect on Matthew 6:25-34.

As you look back, can you recall a specific time when a very real need was graciously met by your good Father?

Describe a time when God taught you a lesson in humility as well as gratefulness, and take time to thank Him for that lesson.

"I lift my eyes to the mountains—where does my help come from? My help comes from the LORD, the Maker of heaven and earth." Psalms 121:1-2 (NIV)

As many married people know, marriage comes with both great joy and great challenge! In the midst of raising strong and independent children, we parents can easily find ourselves worn out by the sheer demands of afterschool clubs, sports, teams, and the needs of our children. Having three children, my husband and I are easily outnumbered and really need an Uber driver to help us transport our kids all over town at the same time. Weekends are easily spent at sporting events and/or helping our family on the farm, leaving very little time for date nights or romantic evenings out. Some-times life gets so full of "other things" that romance becomes something you did when you were dating—or first married. Unfortunately, the lull can become the new norm and the new bane for married life.

> **MARRIAGE COMES WITH BOTH GREAT JOY AND GREAT CHALLENGE!**

I remember going shopping with my girlfriend (a rare treat for both of us), and we were sharing bits and pieces of the struggles and challenges of marriage while living through the tween/teen years of parenting. I remember thinking, *You are not alone, sister. That struggle to carve out time for romance, intimacy, and connection to your spouse is real. I want that. I need that. That is missing from my life and my marriage.*

This heavy feeling came over me as I didn't have words to encourage her in her marriage. I didn't have any advice. I didn't know how to "fix" this in my own marriage. I felt the Holy Spirit nudge me (as the time with friends is precious and rare) that I was to be a light of Jesus—and yet I felt so heavy-hearted. We walked into a shoe store looking for a specific pair of sandals. Upon finding them, we scoured the shelves looking for a size 9. *No Luck. No 9's. No Advice. No Hope.* Just then, my sweet friend pointed and said, "Connie, look up!" Above us were rows and rows of the super cute sandal I was hoping to buy. Then it hit me. It was an "Aha!" moment.

"Yes!" I replied excitedly. "That's it. You nailed it! God just said we need to look up. We cannot fix or save our marriages without Him. Look up! You do God—you focus on God, pray and ask for His help—and He will help with your marriage and my marriage."

I know we came for sandals, but honestly, what I found instead was a message of hope. I don't know how to recreate the golden days of dating and exciting romance—but I do know that God can do what I cannot, if only I remember to look up.

(Disclaimer: Sadly, there were no size 9 sandals left . . . but I got more than I bargained for that shopping day!)

What about you?

With the current demands of your life, do you find it difficult to spend quality time with your spouse or loved ones? How would you describe those relationships right now?

Spend some time "looking up" to God, sharing your struggles and waiting for His wisdom.

HIS PRESENCE IN THE DEEP WATERS *by Kelly Newcomb*

"Surely God is my salvation; I will trust and not be afraid. The LORD, the LORD himself, is my strength and my defense; he has become my salvation." Isaiah 12:2 (NIV)

The last year of my life has been hard, and there have been many tears and an aching heart. But as God has enabled me to seek Him, I see more and more moments of blessing and provision in the midst of the pain of life on this earth. Some of them are small and may seem silly, but taken as a whole, they tell the story of a God who knows my every need and is ever mindful of me.

He provided a beautiful home at a reasonable price for my family to land in after the dissolution of my marriage. He provided a generous financial situation so that I didn't have to fear or upheave my kids while I hustled to find a job that would sustain us. He has shown His faithfulness to my girls in sweet friends who have loved, prayed, and encouraged us in our hurt. I've seen His goodness in friends who rallied around us not only in prayer and love but also in divinely practical ways like showing up to sit with me on the divorce day or taking recycling home to their bins when I missed it and was overwhelmed with anxiety and failure. A friend even gave up a Saturday to change my locks, and another spent time and money to go with me to a conference I wanted to attend.

I see His goodness in my girls, who love me with grace and give me so much joy. God has given my daughter a heart for worship that draws us all closer to Him as she positively bathes us in worship music. The gift of our puppy, Tobin, was above and beyond—God showing off His omniscience and wisdom and love. I would never have expected a dog to bring so much love, joy, and comfort. But God knew exactly what we needed and cared even for a little detail like that. Then, God knew that the book of Isaiah was the perfect book for me to study in my women's Bible study this year, that I needed to be reminded over and over of His sovereignty and His care.

Only such a good and powerful and mindful God could create a grateful heart after so much hurt and fear. I am learning every day what it means to fix my eyes upon Jesus, to know that my help comes from the Lord, to be filled with the oil of joy in the midst of the mourning, to see how God longs to be gracious to me and my children, to feel that God is strengthening me and fighting my battles even when I can't see the victory yet.

Not only does He work on my behalf, but He continually reminds me of His care so that I know that I am not alone. The day after my 17-year-old son left home, I saw a beautiful sunset and was so grateful to realize that there was still beauty in the world, even after the ugliness of the night before. The sun had just set, and beneath the brilliant purples, pinks, and oranges, there was a brilliant horizon, and I felt God whisper that there was still brightness ahead. I didn't know the path I was on, but I had peace that God did, and I loved His reminder that He brings light even in the darkest dark.

When I was truly desperate for Him, I began to see His goodness even in the darkest seasons of my life, things I had never imagined walking through. Over the last two years, I have become more and more aware of God's hand and goodness in my life. The book of Isaiah has been chock-full of promises that I have seen revealed in my life on a daily basis. I wouldn't have chosen these trials, but I see that the testing of my faith has produced patience and trust in God in a way that I didn't have before. I am confident that God is completing the good work He started in me. He has enabled me to see some of the ways that He is with me in the fire and to recognize His presence in the deep waters.

For a long time, I didn't really understand what Nehemiah 8:10 meant when it says, "the joy of the LORD is your strength." I am learning that the joy of the Lord looks like seeing His unending and completely trustworthy faithfulness and goodness over and over in my life. It isn't a zap of instantaneous faith and understanding, but a gradual drawing into deeper understanding and knowing as I see Him move over the course of my days.

So, I think this is what the joy of the Lord looks like: when He gives us eyes to see His provision and His care—even when He doesn't remove the hard things we walk through. This is what it means when Isaiah writes, "When you pass through the waters, I will be with you; and when you pass through the rivers, they will not sweep over you. When you walk through the fire, you will not be burned; the flames will not set you ablaze" (Isaiah 43:2, NIV).

What about you?

Are you passing through some deep waters right now? Take some time to read these promises in Isaiah and rest in His goodness, love, and faithfulness: Isaiah 12:2, 41:10, 41:13, 43:2, 50:7, 54:4.

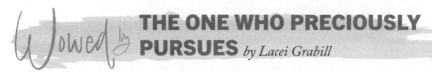

THE ONE WHO PRECIOUSLY PURSUES *by Lacei Grabill*

"But the Lord replied to her, 'Martha, Martha, you are worried and bothered and anxious about so many things; but only one thing is necessary, for Mary has chosen the good part [that which is to her advantage], which will not be taken away from her.'" Luke 10:41-42 (AMP)

Jesus stands at the door of your heart and preciously pursues you. But God doesn't just pursue you for salvation, for your adoption into His family. He also pursues you for relationship. That statement in itself should blow your mind.

The One who spoke the universe into existence pursues a close, personal relationship with you. (If that didn't just make you pause, go back and read that sentence again.) This loving God who desires relationship with people is what makes Christianity different from all other major world religions. Only in Christianity is there a God who can be known by people and who desires to know them so much that He gave His life to make that relationship possible. His love is so great that He is even willing to speak to us in many different unique ways.

He speaks to us through His Word. He speaks to us through others. He speaks to us through His sweet, still voice—those thoughts in your head that you know are so good or so challenging that you didn't put them there yourself. He even sometimes speaks to us through dreams and visions.

Last year, I had a really strange, but stressful dream about being in another country (which very much resembled the country of India). Merchants lined the streets, their colorful booths jutting right up against each other. The sound of their voices filled the warm humid air as they strongly encouraged the people passing by to stop and buy their merchandise. In this dream, I was attempting to do some shopping myself, but I apparently owed someone some money. So, I kept opening this big box of money that I was carrying and counting it in order pay back my debt. However, I never seemed to be able to count it correctly or have the right coins.

I knew I had a flight to catch and was supposed to meet a group of people inside the airport (which was within walking distance), but I couldn't seem to be released to meet them until I had this money counted. As I tried repeatedly to count the money, people talked to me and complimented me on my bracelets, asking if I would like to buy this or that. Suddenly, it dawned on me that counting this money in an open place was not a good idea, so I moved to a more secluded bench and sat down to try to count it once again. But almost immediately, two men walked up, and while one took the money in my hands, the other took the entire money box. As they ran away, I yelled that they were taking my money, but no one seemed to care.

I quickly ran to the airport, found my husband, and tearfully told him what had happened. But, to my surprise, all he did was ask me if I had my passport and ticket. Feeling a bit undervalued and disappointed in his reaction, I coldly informed him that I didn't know the exact location of either of those items. He stared at me in both shock and disbelief, and then he softly mentioned that he had checked the location of his passport and ticket every day of the trip. After stifling the urge to sarcastically congratulate him on his diligence, I opened my purse. It was at that moment that I was hit with the realization of just how important those two items were. I frantically began searching my purse, and then, I woke up.

With my heart still pounding from the stress of the dream, I asked the Lord if the dream was from Him. Almost immediately, I sensed Him say, "You are worried about a lot of things, but only one is necessary. Focus on that. Don't get caught up in details that don't matter. You will never pay me back what you owe me by doing everything right. Just be. Just breathe. Just rest. Just live in my presence and in my pleasure." It was exactly what I needed to hear in that season of my life—a season of too much worry, too many burdens, and too little trust.

Praise God that He preciously pursues us for a deeper relationship with Him. May He help us to slow down enough to hear Him, and to choose the One who is worth all of our focus.

What about you?

Have you opened the door of your heart to the One who preciously pursues you? If so, recall that memory, write it down, and praise Him for His gift of salvation and grace.

Are you caught up in details that don't matter, not choosing the one thing that is necessary, "that which is to your advantage"? Ask God to search your heart for the answer.

How are you actively pursuing a deeper relationship with Him? How have you grown in your closeness to Him in the last year, the last month?

Wowed by HIS SURPRISE
by Karen Grabill

"Some men came, bringing to him a paralyzed man, carried by four of them. Since they could not get him to Jesus because of the crowd, they made an opening in the roof above Jesus by digging through it and then lowered the mat the man was lying on. When Jesus saw their faith, he said to the paralyzed man, 'Son, your sins are forgiven.'" Mark 2:3-5 (NIV)

As most expectant parents, we were anxiously awaiting the birth of our next child. We were trusting God for a normal, healthy, full-term baby. Since this delivery was going to be a scheduled C-section, the obstetrician even asked us to choose the day in the particular week that we felt was the safest. My husband decided he would prefer Wednesday. That way he could go to church that evening for the mid-week service and tell everyone about our new baby (the gender, name, weight, and all the details).

Our baby daughter Kristi Lynne arrived—an answer to our prayers. She was healthy, beautiful, perfect (in our minds) and even had a gentle, quiet spirit to top it off. We were praising the Lord! But after a few months, I began to notice that in the mornings, Kristi would wake up with a discharge in one of her eyes. At first, I just cleaned her face and didn't allow myself to push any alarm buttons in my mind.

However, as time went on, I noticed that although I had brought her dressed perfectly and looking beautiful for church each week, when I'd pick her up from the nursery, her eyes would look nasty. I knew it was time to check with the pediatrician. Unfortunately, he informed us that our baby had a blocked tear duct, and that surgery would be needed to correct the problem.

My heart sank. With sadness and some anxiety, we made an appointment with the pediatric surgeon. But, while awaiting the designated appointment, God showed up! Of course, we were praying for Him to show up, but I'm afraid I really didn't have a high level of faith at that time.

It happened one particular Sunday morning. When I picked Kristi up from the nursery, I noticed that her eye was dry, not matted as usual. Otherwise, nothing seemed out of the ordinary. The same thing occurred at her nap time. I was beginning to wonder why. I **MY HEART SANK.** figured by after the evening service (we had night services in those days), the eye would be showing the usual signs of discharge.

However, to my surprise, her eye was dry once again.

By now this "woman of little faith" (me) was really inquisitive. The following Sunday, one week after no signs of a blocked tear duct, I found the particular lady who had been caring for Kristi in the nursery the week before. I asked her what had happened last Sunday morning in the nursery.

The "woman of faith" (nursery worker) shared that she was just walking around holding our baby, and she decided that Kristi shouldn't have that eye problem any longer. She said she JUST prayed and asked the Lord to heal her. I explained to her that Kristi's eye had been dry and normal for a week, and we celebrated God's goodness together. Hallelujah, God had answered that prayer!

My husband and I decided to keep the appointment with the surgeon to verify this miracle that we were sure had happened. He examined Kristi and said he could see evidence that there had been a blocked tear duct, but it wasn't blocked now, and she wouldn't be needing any type of surgery.

I was so thankful to have a friend who was willing to step out in faith for my need. When I didn't have enough faith for my daughter's healing, my friend had faith. It reminds me of the four friends of the paralytic of Capernaum in Mark 2. They couldn't get their disabled friend to Jesus because the house was too crowded, so they broke a hole in the roof and lowered him down through it right in front of Jesus. May we be the kind of friend that is willing to have that kind of faith for another's need.

What about you?

Am I willing to be the conduit that God chooses to use to pray in faith for a miracle for someone else?

Do I give the same importance to another's needs as I do to my own requests?

MY UNWAVERING GUARD
by Jiyoung Kim

"Indeed, he who watches over Israel never slumbers or sleeps." Psalms 121:4 (NLT)

Psalms 121 is one of the songs from the Song of Ascents for Israel. Thus, this famous psalm was probably sung by the Israelite pilgrims during the journey to the great feasts at Jerusalem. Whenever I read this psalm, I think of the tender but desperate hearts of the ancient pilgrims who were longing for God's very presence at His temple. If I dare say, I believe verse four of Psalms 121 is the highlight of the entire Song of Ascents. The psalmist is so assured that the Father God of Israel is decisively watching over His people at all times. Israel could lose her foot, or fall into the darkness, but her Guard (the One who watches over Israel) neither slumbers nor sleeps!

Ever since I was young, I have kept one unforgettable story in my heart. It is the story of how a father took care of his baby daughter in the children's hospital intensive care unit. The baby was barely breathing. She was on an IV and getting cared for by many nurses. Because the baby was so fragile, the only spot where the doctor could inject an IV needle was the baby's forehead. Thankfully, the doctor was a very skillful man, so he was able to situate the IV needle in the exact place. Careful attention was needed for the baby during the night, in case she moved.

THE BABY WAS BARELY BREATHING.

In the middle of the night, the nurses were surprised to notice that the baby's father did not move at all but stood with the posture of military guard. His eyes were on his baby girl at all times, and he gave her his sole attention. He stood there in the same posture all night long until the baby girl was safely discharged from the unit in the morning. The shocked nurses exclaimed, "What a father!"

The father was my father; the baby girl was me. "You were too valued by your father and me. You are still valued by us so much," my mother said whenever she recalled this episode. This story echoes throughout my life, especially whenever I face diffi-

"YOU WERE TOO VALUED BY YOUR FATHER AND ME."

cult circumstances. When I encounter unexpected and challenging troubles from time to time, I can just picture that my Heavenly Father is unwaveringly guarding me with His sole attention. The Father who guards me never slumbers or sleeps.

If my own father did that when I was so small, fragile and helpless, how much more will my Heavenly Father do when I feel fearful and broken?

In a physical sense and a spiritual sense, I too am a pilgrim who longs for a true home since I live far away from my own country. Therefore, I ascend. I go on this journey to the city of God, "the heavenly homeland" (Heb. 11:16) just as the ancient pilgrims did. Just as they were longing for God's very presence at His temple, I do as well. A Song of Ascents still ascends to His throne by His pilgrims. So does my praise-song.

What about you?

Take time to share a story with someone today of when God guarded you, and shower Him with praises of sheer gratitude for His protection.

Are you a pilgrim in this world, journeying to find the true Home where your Father's sweet presence is? If so, would you let your song ascend at this moment? Sing out your praise song!

HIS NUDGE
by Wendy Elarton

"Yet I am always with you; you hold me by my right hand. You guide me with your counsel, and afterward you will take me into glory." Psalms 73:23-24 (NIV)

Just recently my husband and I were making our way back down the east side of our mitten state. We planned to go through a town that had old memories for us. We had come to minister in a church in that town just after we had finished up at North Central Bible College. Being married for only ten months and ready to be in "full-time ministry" was so exciting and scary, but our great desire to bring youth to Jesus was moving our hearts. We had felt the "nudge" of the Holy Spirit to move to this town after our first of two interviews. We were excited to be in our home state and to serve this church and community.

But first we had to finish school and give our notices of finished employment in Minneapolis. The day came for us to pack our small apartment and say goodbye to our dear classmates and friends. That last night in the apartment we were so excited to be going to our first youth pastor position, we couldn't sleep and decided to leave early in the morning. The drive was uneventful at first until we reached the beautiful (but cold and snowy) upper peninsula of Michigan.

> **OUR GREAT DESIRE TO BRING YOUTH TO JESUS WAS MOVING OUR HEARTS.**

Snow was falling fiercely, and we found ourselves stuck in Escanaba's city park with our little moving truck and car towed on the back. With no phone, no extra cash, and in an unfamiliar place, we were grateful when a man with a big Chevy truck came by. He was happy to pull us out of the snow bank (and to share with us that a Chevy was way better than a Ford). We offered to pay, but our knowledge about his wonderful truck was all he wanted. We were so blessed and happy.

We resumed our trek so thankful and at peace that God had sent someone to take care of us. We then turned the radio on to hear the weather report for our destination. We were shocked to hear the Mackinaw Bridge was closed due to high winds and snow. Our destination was over that bridge. We continued to drive, knowing we had no credit card and only enough gas money to get us to our destination. We knew we would need to spend the night somewhere as it got darker if the storm did not let up.

I still remember the sign for the Howard Johnson's in Manistique, Michigan.

Nathan decided to go in and see what they had available for a cheap price. As I waited prayerfully, I prepared myself to sleep in the truck if needed. We were already super tired from staying up all night. Soon, Nathan came out and told me what had just happened.

The man behind the counter asked him where he was going and why. Nathan proceeded to tell him our story of being Bible college students going to our first appointment of full-time ministry. With no fanfare, the man reached under the counter and tossed Nathan a room key and said, "No charge." As we unloaded our things and walked into the warm room, I was moved to tears for the way God had provided such a comfortable place for us to stay.

After we had settled in a little bit, there was a knock at the door. A nice man from the hotel handed Nathan a Tony's pizza and said, "I thought you might be hungry since everything is closed in town." We were amazed and so thankful for that pizza. The next day, we felt refreshed and prepared to finish our adventure to our new station of ministry. We took the key back to the desk and thanked them again.

God's hand of guidance's that day taught us an important lesson of how He would take care of us if we were willing to be obedient. We didn't know then but nine months later, we would feel that "nudge" to move again, and we would begin the hard task of seeking where God would want us to go. His wisdom and loving guidance led us to a place that we call "the grounds of learning hands-on ministry and healing."

Our Father always knows what we need before we even need to ask and has already set things up. We just need to look up, trust His guidance, and obey His nudges.

What about you?

Make a list of some times in your life when you felt the "nudge" of the Holy Spirit. What happened when you obeyed them? What happened when you didn't?

Has God ever "nudged" someone else to take care of you or to share something significant with you? Take time today to make a phone call, send a text, or write a letter to that person, thanking him or her for obeying His "nudge."

"Consider it pure joy, my brothers and sisters, whenever you face trials of many kinds, because you know that the testing of your faith produces perseverance. Let perseverance finish its work so that you may be mature and complete, not lacking anything." James 1:2-4 (NIV)

This verse is a hard one to live out. When I am met with "trials," I must confess that my first response is not one of pure joy. In actuality, my first emotions are usually confusion and frustration, followed with questions like "Why me, God?" and "When will You take this away?" But, according to this scripture, trials aren't all bad. In fact, if we walk through them with the right attitude and with faith, they can create a wonderful character trait called perseverance that can help us grow in our spiritual maturity. However, despite these gifts that trials can bring, it's still difficult to celebrate them—especially when the trial is happening to your child.

My son, Eric, has always been my kid who struggles with strange health issues. As a baby, he dealt with severe ear infections on a regular basis, and his eardrums actually burst a couple of times. As a little guy, he had a terrible rash on his arms and legs that no one seemed **"WHY ME, GOD?"** to be able to diagnose, and he was often covered in band-aids from him unknowingly scratching the bumps during the night. As he got older, he struggled with allergies, daily stomach aches, and migraines. On top of all that, once he started playing sports, he usually had some type of injury from a game. Random pain and illness were, unfortunately, simply a part of his life.

So, when Eric came to me at fourteen and told me he was feeling dizzy a lot, I didn't think much about it. I figured it was just another one of his weird health problems, and it would eventually go away. But, as the dizziness got worse, and he began to take naps every day and complain about not seeing clearly, I decided to take him in to get checked out. The doctor prescribed some anti-motion meds and a patch he wore behind his ear, but neither of those helped. We were referred to a specialist who gave us exercises to move the crystals in his ear, but that didn't work either.

Then, we made a trip to the University of Michigan to see an audiologist who did numerous tests and referred us to vestibular therapy—which we tried for months to no avail. We tried chiropractors and physical therapy (as they thought it might be a neck issue), but nothing changed the way he was feeling. We saw the optometrist who said his prescription was fine. After waiting for months to get into a pediatric neurologist, we received no answers once again, but he prescribed some medication to try. However, after reading the extreme side effects and praying, I didn't have a peace about giving it to my teenager.

Despite all our appointments with many medical professionals, not one could find anything that was wrong with Eric or anything to help his dizziness. He continued to try to do normal life, but he was tired all the time, and reading caused him to feel worse—which made doing homework a bit difficult. During basketball season, I remember him telling me that it was kind of hard to shoot the ball when he saw two rims!

We continued to pray and ask the Lord for healing and for wisdom. We asked our prayer team to pray over him for healing, as well as the staff and board at our church. Yet, no answers or healing came. Honestly, I became very discouraged and struggled in the waiting; it had now been a whole year since Eric had started to feel this way.

One day, my son mentioned he was having trouble seeing the board at school. Assuming he needed a new prescription for his contacts, I took him in to see his optometrist—a kind man who knew the Lord and was very concerned about Eric's condition. As the doctor examined Eric, I silently cried out to the Lord: *Lord, will you please give this doctor Your wisdom right now? Will you please help him notice something that no one else has noticed?*

YET, NO ANSWERS OR HEALING CAME.

All of a sudden, the doctor stopped the exam, sat back in his chair, and turned to me. He said, "This isn't a problem with Eric's prescription. It's a problem with the ability of his eyes to focus together. I think you need to go see someone who specializes in vision therapy, and I believe this could help his dizziness."

Hopeful and grateful for an answer, we made an appointment for Eric to see this specialist who FINALLY discovered the problem: He has a condition called binocular dysfunction (meaning that one of his eyes has a tendency to overfocus and turn inward, making it difficult for his eyes to send a clear message to his brain.) After months of vision therapy with daily eye exercises, he has experienced a significant improvement. Praise Jesus!

Eric still does his vision exercises most days, and although I don't know why God hasn't completely healed him yet, I do know that the waiting has produced good things in him (and in me). Because he's gone through this trial, Eric knows his need for Jesus. He knows that Mom and Dad can't fix everything—no matter how much they want to. He has learned to Whom he should ultimately run for help when life is hard and overwhelming.

As Christian moms, our biggest prayer for our children is that they will grow up to be strong, godly men and women who love Jesus with all their hearts. Unfortunately, in order for that to happen, they will have to endure some hard times. Our children must go through some times of pain and waiting. No mama wants to hear that, but a life of ease does not produce strong children. We all (including our precious kiddos) need some friction to smooth off our rough edges and to remind us of our desperate need for Him.

I DO KNOW THAT THE WAITING HAS PRODUCED GOOD THINGS IN HIM (AND IN ME).

So, let's consider it pure joy when those seasons of waiting and trials come. The benefits far outweigh the hardships.

What about you?

Spend some time in prayer for the children in your life. Remember they don't just need our prayers that they will be happy, blessed, and successful. Sometimes we have to pray some hard prayers if we truly desire for our children to grow up to be strong men and women of the Lord.

Wowed by THE PROMISE KEEPER
by Christa Krohn

"The Lord is not slow in keeping his promise, as some understand slowness. Instead he is patient with you, not wanting anyone to perish but everyone to come to repentance." 2 Peter 3:9 (NIV)

"You should hear from the doctor in a couple of days. This is something you should be concerned about." Those words were ringing in my ears and sucking the breath out of me as I made my way home from a follow-up pelvic ultrasound. My doctor had been keeping an eye on a small mass that he found during a routine physical. I had always prided myself on being someone who did not panic easily, who trusted the Lord at all times.

But as I waited to hear what the doctor had to say, I did not sleep for two nights. Every fear I ever had about dying young and leaving my children without a mother bombarded my mind. I would swing back and forth between trusting the Lord and total panic. *What if I die? What if I have to take chemo? What if I need surgery?* The "what if's" were driving me crazy. Fear was crowding out His Word. I was having trouble concentrating enough to even meditate on His promises.

Two days later, I heard from the doctor who said, "I am sending you to an oncologist surgeon. Chances are that you have ovarian cancer, and even if you don't, the mass still needs to be removed." I could hardly sleep again that evening. At that point, even trusting the Lord to get me through surgery was beyond me. I was so disappointed in myself. I thought, *Why can't you calm yourself down? Why can't you just trust the Lord?*

THE "WHAT IF'S" WERE DRIVING ME CRAZY.

The next morning as I was walking past the receptionist desk of the church where I worked, I saw a Bible sitting on it. It looked familiar. I opened it up and saw my name written inside. It was a Bible that I had lost three years before. *Where had it come from? How did it just show up out of the blue?* I took that Bible home that night, knowing that this could not be just a coincidence.

Before I opened it, I shared with the Lord how disappointed I was in myself for not being able to stand on His Word and find peace over the last few days. I heard Him say that He had seen my struggle, and He was not going to leave me there. He said, "My promises had to track you down." He had caused that Bible to show up after all these years because He knew there was a promise in it that I had underlined, and I needed to see it in that moment.

Excitement built as I opened my Bible. I found that I had underlined 2 Peter 3:9 and dated it "2009." In the margin, I had written comments that spoke of letting go of disappointment in unanswered prayers and trusting that He was going to heal me. I was stunned. He led me to another verse that I had underlined. It was a promise that He had given me the very first time I dealt with the fear of dying young and leaving my children without a mother.

It was Psalms 91:15-16: "He will call upon me, and I will answer him; I will be with him in trouble, I will deliver him and honor him. With long life I will satisfy him and show him my salvation" (NIV). God was promising to heal me—that whatever the outcome from the surgery, it would not lead to death. That was the only healing I thought He was talking about. I had no idea what He had in store for me. In that moment, the fear of death left, and even

HE SAID, "MY PROMISES HAD TO TRACK YOU DOWN."

though the days that followed were not easy, I never had trouble fighting fear with His Word again.

The day for the surgery came, and the Lord told me (as I prepared to leave for the hospital) that there would be a shout of victory in the camp before the day was over. And there was! It was not cancer. It was one of the worst cases of endometriosis the surgeon had ever seen. I had never been diagnosed with that before. The Lord brought healing to my body by the removal of the endometriosis that had been causing trouble in my digestive system for over 30 years.

Looking back at the margins of 2 Peter, I realized that I had written those comments when I was going through some significant testing for digestive issues.

I HAD NO IDEA WHAT HE HAD IN STORE FOR ME.

For years, I had felt sick every time I ate. I had written those words in the margin because I believed that the Lord was finally going to heal me from those digestive struggles. Interestingly, He did not heal me in 2009, but nine years later he had that promise TRACK me

down. He USED that promise to give me peace. He FULFILLED that promise through a dreaded cancer scare and hysterectomy. I praise the Promise Keeper who answered a prayer for healing that I had been praying for 30 years in a way I never saw coming—since that surgery, I no longer feel sick when I eat!

If the Lord has spoken a promise to you from His Word, you can believe Him. It doesn't matter if He spoke it yesterday or ten years ago. Time does not nullify His promise. He will bring it to pass in His time and in His way.

What about you?

Spend some time today reminding yourself of the promises and words God has spoken over your life and has already fulfilled. Let them build faith in the Promise Keeper.

Then, pray you will trust Him more with the promises you've yet to see fulfilled. Speak Isaiah 55:11 over the situations and rest in His character: "So is my word that goes out from my mouth; it will not return to me empty, but will accomplish what I desire and achieve the purpose for which I sent it." (NIV)

HIS DELIVERANCE
by Danielle Spencer

"The thief comes only to steal and to kill and destroy; I have come that they may have life, and have it to the full. "John 10:10 (NIV)

I always wanted to be married. But I wanted to wait for the man God willed for me to marry. I started dating a guy who I thought could be the one God had for me. However, there were red flags of warning even before we officially started dating. I chose to ignore all of them. As the relationship continued, there was nothing about it that was good. More red flags kept popping up.

My mom and sister tried to tell me, tried to point things out that were not good at all. I chose to ignore everything they said. Because of that, the relationships I had with them, which had always been strong, were beginning to suffer. God also gave me dreams, making it clear to me that I should not be in that dating relationship. I chose to ignore those too. So many things I had been saving for my future husband were being given away. Yet, I was not being treasured, respected, or loved.

Eventually, I started to allow myself to see what was really happening. It was then that I went to the altar at church. As I prayed and cried, I said, "God, I feel like my life is falling apart, and I need You to put it back together." God is so faithful! He gave me a vision, making it clear that He was living inside me and roaring like a lion. He was fighting off the attacks and the army of the enemy. Things really started changing (even more) when I had yet another vision from God. In that one, He was still roaring and fighting for me, but at the same time, a shout rose up in me. I

YET, I WAS NOT BEING TREASURED, RESPECTED, OR LOVED.

was ready to be on the offense and to choose to be who God created me to be.

After that, I decided to give that relationship a break. But inside I knew it was going to be over. When the break was finished, I ended the relationship. It wasn't easy, but it was so freeing! God delivered me out of that relationship. He delivered me out of a place I should not have been. He restored the relationships I had with my mom and sister. He brought healing to me.

Around that time, I heard someone pray for God's perfect will, not His permissible will. I knew that was exactly what I wanted! I wanted God's perfect will for my life. As I mentioned before, I had always desired to be married. Fully surrendering that desire to the Lord was difficult for me. I didn't want to surrender and end up not getting married.

God brought me to the place of fully surrendering to Him, of trusting Him, of knowing that His will is the absolute best—whatever it is. I finally decided to truly surrender my life and my desires to God, to His will, whether that meant I would get married someday or not. What I didn't know is that my future husband had also grown to a place of truly surrendering to the Lord and His will around the same time.

Soon after that I started talking to a friend at church. I had known him for about two and a half years, but we had only ever been friends. During that conversation, God physically changed my vision, and I started seeing him differently. Little did I know that during the same conversation, God also started working in him. Only God could have done that! We started courting (dating with the intent of marriage) very soon after.

Our relationship was (and still is) beautiful. He truly loves and lives for the Lord; he treasures me, encourages me, respects me, and challenges me to continue to grow in my relationship with God. While we were courting, we decided to pray and fast one day a week. We also decided to not see or talk to each other on that day. We wanted to pray, to seek God, and to find out His perfect will—without being distracted by each other. In this time, God made it abundantly clear to us that it was His perfect will for us to get married. I am truly blessed to be married to him, the one God has given to me.

God revealed that He delivered me in two ways. First, He delivered me out of where I was not supposed to be. Then, He delivered me to the right place, the right relationship, and His perfect will. His deliverance is one of the beautiful ways He displays His unconditional love for us. I am wowed by Him!

What about you?

What is something you've had to surrender to the Lord that was really hard for you? What happened when you surrendered it?

What are the differences between a relationship in which you are treasured and cherished and one in which you are not?

HIS ALWAYS-ON-TIME GRACE
by Christina Shafer

"But He said to me, "My grace is sufficient for you, for my power is made perfect in weakness." 2 Corinthians 12:9 (NIV)

As a young woman, I was asked to help co-lead a youth mission trip to Guatemala. I had never been there before. I was also asked to pray about speaking to a group of pastors and leaders at one of the events. It was going to be televised, and I would speak to them with an interpreter. I remember feeling so excited—and inadequate and nervous. Yet, I felt God leading me to do it.

I spent weeks praying and preparing for the trip and for this message, yet I never felt led to what I was supposed to share. This was very difficult for me as I like to be prepared days before the actual event. As we arrived in Guatemala, I still did not know exactly what God wanted me to say, but I knew that I had a few more days before I had to share. I would awaken early each morning to prepare and still—nothing.

On the day I was supposed to speak, some members of our team got sick from something we ate the night before. I was sick as well and spent the whole morning in the bathroom. I remember telling the Lord that this must be why I didn't get a message and that I was going to tell the other leader on the trip that I was too sick to share.

At that moment, I heard God speak so clearly: "My grace is sufficient for you and made perfect in your weakness. Get up and prepare. I have the message for you now. You are ready." In an hour's time He told me what to share, and He gave me grace. The whole time preparing and speaking, clear until we got back to the mission house, I did not need to use the bathroom even once. His grace was sufficient!

This had a huge impact on my life. No, I was not miraculously healed from the sickness. I struggled for weeks after the trip ended. Yet I found that His grace and strength are sufficient in the moments when I cannot do anything on my own, and I found that He is never late. He will give me the words to say even if it's an hour before the event. I just need to be obedient and trust Him.

He has used this example in my life many times, reminding me that His grace is sufficient even when things are hard. And He is never late. His timing is perfect, and this whole

I JUST NEED TO BE OBEDIENT AND TRUST HIM.

thing is all about Him. I am just the vessel, ready to do what He wants and trusting He will give me what I need just when I need it.

What about you?

Is there an area of life where you feel like God is late?

What does "His power is made perfect in your weakness" mean for you?

Wowed by THE ONE WHO DELIGHTS IN ME
by BriAnna McGuire

"He brought me out into a spacious place. He rescued me because He delighted in me." Psalms 18:19 (NIV)

This is my favorite verse. He delights in YOU. He has made the heavens, the oceans, the stars in the sky, the galaxies that are beyond our sight, and everything else; yet, He delights in you. I think that is so crazy and makes me feel so loved. Because He delights in you, He rescues you. He rescues you from times of trouble, He protects you, He saves you.

I grew up in a pastor's home. I knew who God was, and I got saved when I was about five years old. I grew up singing songs about how Jesus loves me and about how big God is. I knew stories of David

HE DELIGHTS IN YOU.

and Goliath, Queen Esther, Jonah, Noah, and so many more. I always believed in God and knew He was there for me. However, I struggled.

I battled with insecurity for a long time. I constantly had people watching me, and I always felt pressure to do the perfect thing. God called me into ministry when I was about seven, and I knew at age twelve that I wanted to preach—but I was so afraid to speak. I was afraid that I would say something wrong. I also struggled with thinking I was too young to speak yet, or that I always heard God wrong.

Every summer for four years I went on a choir tour in Arkansas and loved every minute of it. When I went the summer after my junior year, I did not know how much my life was about to change. On July 11, we were praying in one of the churches for the service, and I felt like God was telling me to do something, but I kept saying to Him, "God, tell someone else. I can't do that. What if I am not hearing you correctly?" Then, all of the sudden, one of my friends walked up and said, "I feel like God is telling you that He has given you mighty words to speak, so speak them. He wants to use you."

I WAS AFRAID I WOULD SAY SOMETHING WRONG.

In that moment I broke down, and I surrendered myself to Him completely. I gave Him all of my insecurity and doubt; I wanted to be used by Him. After that, I gained confidence, and I stopped living in so much fear. I began to seek Him in a new way, and I was open to being used by Him.

Do I still struggle with insecurities sometimes? Yes. I am human. However, I know that God has called me to places that are out of my reach, and I have to trust Him. I know that He has made me the exact way that He wants me, and I have to be confident in that.

I am so grateful that God rescued me from my own harmful thoughts. As he delights in me, so I delight in myself.

What about you?

Have you ever battled or are you currently battling insecurity?

Every day, think good things about yourself. Remind yourself to Whom you belong and in Whom your identity is found.

Wowed by THE GOD OF THE IMPOSSIBLE
by Donna Stocker

"Jesus looked at them and said, 'With man this is impossible, but not with God; all things are possible with God.'" Mark 10:27 (NIV)

Velma's background was one of nightclubs, drugs, addictions, and a prison stay. She lived in Las Vegas for years, and she was in a relationship with our son, Ben. Velma called her parents after giving birth to our granddaughter Maliya and asked if they would come and get them. Although Velma's relationship with her parents was nonexistent up to that time, her parents agreed to come for the sake of the baby.

Several months passed. Velma confessed she was struggling and using drugs. We began to pray and felt the Holy Spirit challenging us to ask ourselves if we were supposed to just pray or be part of the answer. We called Velma and extended the invitation that if she was ready to change, we would take her to an addiction rehab center called Teen Challenge. We knew that she could find Jesus there—the One who has the power to forgive and bring deliverance. We prayed, waited, and finally (praise the Lord), the call came. We made arrangements to pick Velma up at her parent's house. They said she was hopeless and didn't think it was possible that she would ever change.

On the way to pick her up, we prayed and listened to worship music in the car. One of the songs proclaimed, "With God anything is possible." These specific words were sung over and over. I said to my husband that I felt we were supposed to share that song with Velma's parents. We arrived at their house and found Velma in bad shape. You could feel the contempt in the home. We spoke directly to Velma's parents and told them that this was a good plan, and with Jesus in her life, it was possible to change.

They continued to shake their heads declaring, "Not Velma. Impossible!" We asked if we could play them the song, and they agreed. As they heard the words "with God anything is possible," you could see the Holy Spirit softening their hard hearts. By the end of the song, they were crying. We prayed together and spoke over them, encouraging them to give God a chance because with Him anything is possible.

In one year's time, Velma came into salvation, deliverance from drugs and addictions, was water baptized, and filled with the Holy Spirit. Upon Velma's graduation from Teen Challenge, we were concerned that if she went back to Illinois, she might not be strong enough to stand in her new faith. Once again, we were challenged: *Was prayer enough or were we to be a part of the answer?* We felt the Holy Spirit urging us to invite Velma and Maliya to live with us for at least one year to solidify what God has done in her life. When we presented this offer to her, she was excited. She had learned the Bible story of Naomi and Ruth. She readily accepted our offer, claiming she needed a Naomi in her life. I became Velma's Naomi, and Velma became my Ruth for the next year and a half.

About one year after Velma and Maliya were on their own, Velma married our son Ben, Maliya's father. They married in the month of October. By the next summer, Velma wasn't feeling well. She had been to a doctor a few times without much concern. By mid-July, Velma was so sick she was hospitalized. Tests were run, and Velma was diagnosed with stage four colon cancer. Thirteen days later, Velma passed away on her birthday, August 1, 2016 at the age of 44.

Velma's family saw the difference Jesus made in her life. She was active in her church and sang in the choir. She became a responsible parent, had a job, and finished her BA degree. Her sister and brother-in-law came to know the Lord. Velma's parents experienced a new understanding of Jesus. In fact, we even had the joy of taking her parents to Israel and baptizing her father in the Jordan River. Maliya is being raised by Velma's sister and husband in the ways of the Lord.

A few days before Velma passed, she sat up in her hospital bed and gave a strong profession of faith by declaring, "If God is ready to meet me, I am ready to meet him." Velma's life after meeting Jesus was filled with surpassing victories. Romans 8:37 (AMP) tells us that "we are more than conquerors and gain a surpassing victory through Him who loved us." Her life was proof that with God all things are possible!

I look forward to the day when we will be together again. I say this back to my Ruth who is enjoying the ultimate victory—eternity with Jesus: "Where you go I will go, and where you stay I will stay" Ruth 1:16 (NIV). I am so thankful to have answered the Holy Spirit's challenge to not only pray but be willing to be part of the answer in Velma's life. I humbly, with gratitude, GIVE GOD ALL THE GLORY!

What about you?

Can you recall times when God used you to be part of His answer? Take a moment to pray this prayer: "Oh Lord, may the ears of my spirit be tuned to Your voice so I don't miss opportunities to partner with You for a display of Your glory."

Wowed by THE PERFECT PROVIDER
by Glenda Olson

"And God is able to bless you abundantly, so that in all things at all times, having all that you need, you will abound in every good work." 2 Corinthians 9:8 (NIV)

I stood on the top step breathing in the sweet smell of plumerias, looking down beyond my classroom to the beautiful ocean beyond. As I stared out at the horizon, once again my heart filled with gratitude for all God had done for me. For the past nine months I had been blessed to be a part of an intensive Bible study school. God taught me so much. In fact, when I talk about that time in my life, the only way I can describe it is that He did a complete brain surgery on me. He replaced my old way of thinking with the truth, grace, and love that is found in His amazing Word. I was so deeply in love with Him and with His Word, and all I wanted to do was to go share all that I had learned.

Our class was given an opportunity to go on an outreach overseas to teach others how to study God's word (in a country where there are very few Christians and opportunities to do so). I knew I wanted to go, and through prayer, I knew I was called to go. I committed to going but I had one small problem: I didn't have sufficient funds for the trip. Still, I knew I was meant to go, so I just knew that He would make a way. I was able to walk in this tremendous faith because of the examples of leaders around me. I think specifically of two stories the founders of the Bible school shared with me.

In one of them, the husband shared how all he wanted to do was to take his wife out on a date. They were living as missionaries in Asia, and he had zero money. Yet, he knew they needed a date, so he prayed and asked God to provide for it. That very day, he received a card in the mail from a supporter back in the US. In the card, she wrote how the Lord had pressed upon her heart to send him a card with one dollar in it, and though she thought it a bit silly, she obeyed, and here it was. She hoped it was what he needed. Little did she know it was exactly what he needed, for where they were stationed, that was just what it cost to take his wife out for a treat! God perfectly provided for their date.

Another story shared with me was how one year this founding couple was challenged to ask God how much money to give away that year. They prayed and were shocked to hear the amount He was leading them to give away. It was more than the total amount of their support as missionaries. They took that amount to the Lord and committed that if those funds came to them, they would offer it back to Him. At the end of that year, sure enough, they had enough support for their mission work as well as the amount He had asked them to give away, which they joyfully did. He perfectly provided for their audacious giving!

Fast forward to the week before I was to leave on my mission trip. I had some of the necessary funds but still found myself $1400 short. And yet, I knew I was supposed to go. I had my plane ticket, and I kept praying and moving forward each day, getting ready to leave. I admit that as I got closer and closer to my departure date, I started to hear that little voice of doubt: *Is He really going to provide so you can go on this trip? Maybe you aren't meant to go! Maybe it is too dangerous! Maybe you won't even be a good teacher and they don't need you!* I had just gone through the most beautiful time of soaking in God's word of my life, so I knew that this voice of doubt was not His. I rebuked the enemy in the name of Jesus, and that sly chatter quieted. And in that quiet place I felt Him whisper to my heart, "I called you, and I will provide for you to do this good work." That was all I needed. I believed Him.

Two days before we left, I went to check my mail, and I saw that I had a letter from my sending church back home. My eyes tear up even now as I remember the words I read in their note. They said that a few weeks ago they had taken a love offering for their overseas missionaries because they felt led to send us an extra gift of funds. My hands trembled as I turned the check over, and then the tears flowed. There in my shaking hands was a check for $1407. Not only did He provide the remaining funds I needed to pay for my trip, but there was seven extra dollars! He provided above and beyond because seven dollars could (and did) buy a lot of Cokes and treats on that trip! He perfectly provided for my mission trip.

On that trip, I ended up getting connected with the ministry I was to work with the next few years, and through it I also ended up meeting my amazing husband, Mike. You can only imagine how grateful I am that I trusted Him as my perfect Provider and that I walked in faith when He called me to go.

What about you?

Can you think of a time He perfectly provided for you? Take a moment to thank Him for what He did and then ask if there is anyone who needs to be encouraged by hearing your story. If there is something He is asking you to do or give for His kingdom, obey and believe for His perfect provision.

THE GOD WHO HEARS
by Kyja Malone

"Answer me when I call, O God of my righteousness! You have given me relief when I was in distress. Be gracious to me and hear my prayer!" Psalm 4:1 (ESV)

You never think it's going to happen to you until you hear the doctor say that word—"cancer." I can relate to Job when he said in Job 3:25-26, "What I feared has come upon me; what I dreaded has happened to me. I have no peace, no quietness; I have no rest, but only turmoil" (NIV). That was how I felt in that moment. It was literally one of my worst fears coming true.

My husband, Michael, was a healthy man in his mid 30's. We had two young kids, and I was pregnant with our third who was due very soon. Michael had been having pain throughout the summer, but we thought he had just pulled a muscle. The pain continued to get worse. He was losing weight and in constant (and at times intense) pain. He went to the ER, and the doctors discovered that he had a large tumor near his spine that was affecting his nerves. They said it was "likely lymphoma" and that it was "very aggressive."

When I heard those words, all I could do was pray. It was the only thing I knew to do. I cried out to God, begging him not to take away my children's father. I prayed that he would heal Michael. I prayed that Michael would be able to see the birth of this third child I was carrying. But it wasn't just me; there were hundreds of people praying for us during that time. We felt the prayers of peace. We felt the prayers of wisdom. We felt the prayers of joy in the midst of trial. We could feel God answering those prayers during that time.

THE PAIN CONTINUED TO GET WORSE.

One of those answers came when Michael was in the hospital for the first time. He was getting all kinds of tests done to determine exactly what was going on. Meanwhile, I was just a few days away from my due date. We spent the first two days in the hospital praying for healing but also praying for wisdom about our baby's birth. We needed to decide if we should ask the doctor for a c-section (so that we could schedule it around Michael's tests), or if we should just let things happen naturally and risk him not being able to be there.

As we prayed that second night, one of our pastors and his wife came to pray with us, and they reminded us of the time when Jesus was in the boat with His disciples, and there was a storm. Jesus knew that storm was coming. It didn't take Him by surprise, just like our situation didn't come as a surprise to Jesus. He knew, and He had a plan. We decided to take the night to pray about it and make a decision in the morning.

That next morning at 5:15am, my water broke at home! I continued to pray on the way to the hospital because I knew that Michael was scheduled to have several tests that morning, but I really needed him for this! God heard my prayer. Our daughter was born in the middle of the only two-hour time slot that Michael had that day without any tests! He was there for the birth, and he even got to hold our daughter and pray over her. We were able to spend some sweet time together before he had to go.

This was nothing short of a miracle. From those first days in the hospital, God heard our prayers and answered them in such a beautiful and powerful way. He continued to answer prayers over and over again, which is why I can now write that my husband is in remission! God is so faithful and so good.

THIS WAS NOTHING SHORT OF A MIRACLE.

What about you?

Reflect on a time when God answered a prayer you prayed.

What is something you are circling in prayer right now? Don't give up. Continue to circle it in prayer.

Wowed by THE ONE WHO TEACHES US

by Pam Wellington

"I will be with both of you as you speak, and I will instruct you both in what to do." Exodus 4:15b (NLT)

About a year and a half after I was saved, I had the privilege of being mentored by some older women in our small church of believers. Three dear ladies—Carol, Effie and Jean—took to heart the Titus 2:4 Scripture that instructs the older women to train up the younger ones. They began a Bible study for the young moms in our church.

It was Tuesday morning, and the young moms were eager to drop off their children with the female caregiver and get across the hall to begin our Bible study. I was one of those moms, along with my friend, Shawna. Both being new believers, she and I had hit it off immediately, quickly becoming close friends.

Carol would first lead us in praise and worship (a cappella no less). Oh, what precious times those were! Then, she would expound on passages of Scripture that God had "highlighted" for her to share, or she'd teach us on a particular topic or book of the Bible. Effie and Jean shared less frequently but were always there for support and encouragement. Looking back, this was definitely my spiritual training ground. It was here that I learned to pray out loud, read my Bible daily, pray for one another with the laying on of hands, and to move in the gifts of the Spirit in a friendly and safe environment.

OH, WHAT PRECIOUS TIMES THOSE WERE!

Shawna and I soon fell into the routine of going to her house or mine right after Bible study each week. With six children between us, we would then prepare and share lunch together. As our children played nearby, she and I would talk and talk and talk some more about what we had learned that morning, often asking questions of one another.

I vividly recall one day in particular: I stood at Shawna's stove stirring yet another pot of mac and cheese for our kids. Shawna was behind me at the other counter, cutting up fruit. She asked at one point, "How can we tell the difference between condemnation and conviction? Like when do we know if it's God's correction or just the enemy harassing us?"

My immediate thought was, *Great question. I have no idea.* As I turned to tell her this very thing, something completely unexpected came out instead: "The Word says there is no condemnation in Christ, so that clearly comes from the enemy. His motive is to discourage us and add to our load, like laying more bricks on top of the others we're already carrying. When God convicts us, He not only points out what we've done wrong or what He wants corrected, but He also tells us exactly WHAT to do about it." Shawna stared at me with a startled expression and said, "Wow! Your answer was so profound, but I understand it completely."

YOUR ANSWER WAS SO PROFOUND, BUT I UNDERSTAND IT COMPLETELY.

We both shared a laugh when I explained what I had really intended to say. Somehow, we both knew that God had spoken this wisdom, even though it had come out of my mouth. We were so awed by this and felt as though we were standing on holy ground right there on her kitchen linoleum. That day gave us a new insight into the miraculous moving of our God by His Holy Spirit, and it definitely spurred us into desiring to know even more of Him.

What about you?

Recall a time when you recognized that God was speaking through you. How did you know it was Him?

From your experience, what are some differences you've found between conviction and condemnation?

Wowed by MOLDY BERRIES
by Tammy Screws

"I know what it is to be in need, and I know what it is to have plenty. I have learned the secret of being content in any and every situation, whether well fed or hungry, whether living in plenty or in want. I can do all this through him who gives me strength." Philippians 4:12-13 (NIV)

Peanut butter and jelly sandwiches are a favorite of my three kids, but not with just any jelly. They have to be made with my homemade jam! The kids love the fresh, reduced-sugar recipe, and I am happy to make it for them. Each year when the berries are in season and on sale, I will stock up the pantry with jam.

One particularly difficult year, our sense of "normal" seemed to collapse. We were dealing with job loss and the potential of moving, on top of other issues, so the jam making took a backseat. As I assessed the pantry before winter, I told my children we would have enough jam left for one jar a month until the berries were back in season. They immediately began to protest, letting me know that would not be enough jam!

God knows the desires of my kids' hearts. I was on my way home from a doctor's appointment, and I noticed a sign at our family center which read "free bread today," so I stopped. When I got out of the car, I noticed not only bread, but other groceries as well. Then I saw it—an entire pallet of strawberries! Upon closer examination there were two or three moldy berries in each container. I thought then that the berries would either freeze or finish molding overnight, so I grabbed two flats of berries, leaving plenty behind for someone else to rescue.

ONE PARTICULARLY DIFFICULT YEAR, OUR SENSE OF "NORMAL" SEEMED TO COLLAPSE.

When I got home, I threw away all of the moldy berries and then washed and stemmed the rest. My son helped me chop them all up, and I was able to make fifteen more pints of jam—enough to make it through the winter. It took a lot of hard work sorting, washing, stemming, and canning the jam, but it was a blessing from God. I saw it as His way of providing for the wants of my kids and blessing us abundantly.

The following week I met a friend for lunch and shared with her my story of how God blessed us with jam, even though we had to sort through moldy berries.

She called me the following Monday and said she felt as though God asked her to share my story at church on Sunday to remind people to look for Christ's many blessings all around. After church, two people came up to her, gave her cash, and asked her to pass it on to "the lady who made the jam." Wow! Not only did God provide the jam that my kids wanted, but he also provided $1100 which we needed to pay bills that month.

Sometimes in life we can lose sight of the many blessings of God. The fact that we are alive and breathing is reason to praise the Lord! I am still without a job and in the process of moving, but I know that my God shall supply all my needs according to His riches in glory! A good friend of mine once said, "God's account never runs low."

There are many seasons in life, not just berry season. When we were in a season of financial plenty, we were faithful to pay our tithe, to give offerings, and to bless others abundantly as the Lord led. Now in our season of want, we are still faithful to pay our tithe, and to give offerings, and I am grateful to see how God is meeting our needs—including providing the right kind of jam for my kids' pb and j.

What about you?

Read Philippians 4:10-20 and Malachi 3:10. Then reflect on these questions:

Are you walking through a season of financial need right now or have you walked through one in the past? What is or was your attitude towards it?

Have you faithfully been tithing (giving the first ten percent of your income to God through your local church)?

Take time now to thank God for at least five blessings in your life. Then ask Him to help you to recognize His many blessings around you all throughout the day.

Wowed by LOSS
by Lisa Homrich

"If we are thrown into the blazing furnace, the God whom we serve is able to save us. He will rescue us from your power, Your Majesty. But even if He doesn't, we want to make it clear to you, Your Majesty, that we will never serve your gods or worship the gold statue you have set up." Daniel 3:17-18 (NLT)

Have you ever lost something? I mean truly lost it? I'm not talking it's lost, like I can't find it; I'm talking I lost it—like I had it, it was mine, and now it's gone. The loss of a child is unlike any loss I've ever experienced in my life, especially when this loss is due to a miscarriage. One minute you've got this baby growing inside you, the next minute . . . it's gone.

Back in 2014, my husband, David, and I were so excited to find out we were pregnant with our very first child! Being a parent had been a desire of mine for such a long time. David, on the other hand, had finally felt like he was ready.

Finding out you're pregnant is one of the most exciting things, until you get to have your first ultrasound; then THAT becomes the most exciting thing. Or at least that was what I thought—until the day we went to have our first ultrasound. I was about ten weeks pregnant at the time. We were so excited to see our little bundle of joy.

We got into the room and awaited in anticipation. Then we saw it. There on the screen where the baby was supposed to be was a giant black hole. It was the amniotic sac, but there was no baby inside. Our friend, the one who did our ultrasound, hurried to get her instructor and another nurse. The two women looked at the screen, and, in what seemed like only a second, concluded that I was having an ectopic pregnancy.

"I don't know what that means. What is that?" Those are the only words I could manage to get out. Then I just sat there as they explained to me that more than likely the baby was on the outside of the sac. They said this could be very dangerous for both me and the baby. As the nurse and the instructor started to walk away, our friend came over and said to us that she didn't think that was what was going on. She told us she was going to contact my doctor to schedule an emergency ultrasound with her. Then she had us wait outside.

I HAD IT, IT WAS MINE, AND NOW IT'S GONE.

That time of waiting was one of the worst. I couldn't stop crying. So many thoughts were racing through my mind. *Was our baby going to die? Was I going to die? Why was this happening?* As David and I sat there, waiting, we began to do the only thing we knew how to do—we prayed.

Once we got to our emergency appointment with the doctor, I was relieved to hear that it was not an ectopic pregnancy. But the words that came next weren't that much better: "When we look, we see no baby. You're going to have a miscarriage." Instantly my heart dropped into my stomach. I didn't realize until that moment how common miscarriages are. We were told we needed to wait a week to see what happened and then come back for another ultrasound.

I wasn't sure how I'd make it through the week, but David (being the man of God he is) asked our doctor what the likelihood would be of us coming back in a week for another ultrasound and there being a baby. She said that this does happen, though it's not common. When we left that appointment, we continued to pray. We are people of faith, so our prayer went something like this: "Lord, we know You can do all things. We are praying and believing that you can form this baby inside my womb. We are believing for a miracle. But even if you don't, we still trust You."

As I think back on this event in my life, I'm reminded of Shadrach, Meshach and Abednego. They loved the Lord and served Him wholeheartedly. But there came a point when their faith was put to the test. The king at the time, King Nebuchadnezzar, had a statue made in Babylon. Then he commanded everyone who lived in Babylon at the time to bow to the ground (when they heard the sound of the instruments) and worship the statue. Anyone who refused would be thrown into a blazing furnace.

When everyone heard the sound, everyone bowed as they were told—everyone except for Shadrach, Meshach and Abednego. They knew that to worship God meant to worship Him alone. They weren't going to bow down to any other god, statue, or person. I love their response to the king in Daniel 3:17-18. These three men inform the King that they know their God can save them from death in the furnace, BUT EVEN IF HE DOESN'T, they won't bow down.

But even if He doesn't . . . This is exactly how David and I felt. We knew God was able and could do a miracle, but even if He didn't, He was still God, and we would still trust and serve Him. This is the heart and attitude that God desires us to have—a heart and attitude that trusts God's plans so much more than our own. God knew what was best. He had a plan in all of this.

BUT EVEN IF HE DOESN'T . . .

As I look back, I am reminded over and over again of how perfect God's plans are. David and I now have an amazing, compassionate, handsome, smart little boy who is five. He loves the Lord with all of his heart. And even though the Lord didn't choose to stop the miscarriage, and it was painful, we still choose to trust Him. We now realize that we wouldn't have had our son at the time we did, if we wouldn't have experienced what we did. God truly is faithful and works everything out in His perfect timing!

What about you?

Have you had a time in your life when God didn't answer a prayer as you hoped He would? How did you respond?

How can we encourage ourselves to continue to trust "even if He doesn't" do things the way we think they should be done, or when we think they should be done?

Wowed by THE PRECIOUS HOLY SPIRIT
by Gail Duford

"The Lord is my strength and shield. I trust him with all my heart. He helps me, and my heart is filled with joy. I burst out in songs of thanksgiving." Psalms 28:7 (NLT)

It was on a late Sunday afternoon when we had an up-close and personal experience with the precious Holy Spirit. When our son Robbie was only two-and-a-half years old, he began to run a fever. As time passed, he lay in my arms, seemingly in a deep sleep and not moving around at all. Needless to say, my husband Don and I were very concerned for our son.

Don's parents stopped by our house to visit for a bit before going on to church. As they left, they hadn't gone more than one block when the precious Holy Spirit directed them to turn around and drive back to our house. In just those few minutes between them leaving and coming back, Don and I tried to wake up our beloved son, but we were unsuccessful. He just lay limp and feverish in my arms. When my in-laws came back and rang our doorbell, we were relieved to hear them tell us that the Holy Spirit had spoken to them and told them to come back to our home and lay their hands on Robbie and pray for him.

So, in obedience to the Holy Spirit, my husband's father placed his hands on Robbie, and we all prayed to the Lord on his behalf. Immediately after our cries to the Lord our Healer, Robbie came out of that coma-like condition! He still had a fever, but we had the assurance that God had touched our two-and-a-half-year-old. From that moment, Robbie started getting well. As I am writing this today, tears of thanksgiving and gratitude flood over my soul. To God be the glory!

God truly showed Don and me that night, as first-time parents, that we can call out to Him anytime, night or day, twenty-four hours a day, and He will hear our prayers and answer.

What about you?

Have you ever sensed a prompting by the Holy Spirit to pray for someone? How did you know it was from the Lord? How did you respond? How does this story encourage you to obey those promptings?

Wowed by GRASS
by Lacei Grabill

"For he will command His angels concerning you to guard you in all your ways."
Psalms 91:11 (NIV)

I have always loved reading or hearing stories of rescue—whether it be a medieval romance about a damsel in distress or a news story about a lost child who was found. Little did I know that by the time I was eighteen, I would have my own story of rescue.

Keith, my husband, and I (who were dating at the time) had driven with a couple of friends to a youth service in a town that was about two hours away. That night, on the way home from the service, Keith was driving my car (because I am directionally challenged and didn't know the way home). Suddenly, we came to the top of a hill and met an unexpected "T" in the road. It was too late to stop, so we ended up popping the car up onto the median and hitting a sign. After the initial shock was over, we decided the car still seemed safe to drive, so we continued to head home.

Because Keith was still a little shook up from hitting a curb and a sign (with MY car), our friend Chad volunteered to drive the rest of the way. Our other friend, Nicole, got into the passenger seat, which left Keith and me in the backseat. Everything was going fine, until I noticed Chad was driving over the middle line. We were on a two-way highway, and as I started to ask him what was going on, I looked at his hands on the steering wheel. He was literally shaking the wheel from side-to-side yelling, "I have no control over the car. I can't do anything."

As we continued to merge into the lane with oncoming traffic, I saw the lights of a semi headed straight for us. I remember looking out the windshield and thinking, We are all going to die. Suddenly, I felt Keith push me down into the seat, and put himself on top of me, to shield me with his body from the imminent head-on collision. A million thoughts rushed through my mind as I waited for the blare of a horn and the sound of crushing metal. I braced myself for either immense pain or the end of my short life here on earth.

"I HAVE NO CONTROL OVER THE CAR."

But instead of experiencing either of those things, I suddenly felt like I was on a merry-go-round. I realized the car must be spinning, and I anxiously awaited the crash, followed by pain. But there wasn't one. The car skidded to a gentle stop in some tall grass, and Chad opened the door to get some light. Wide-eyed, we all stared at each other, and we quickly discovered that none of us were injured in any way—not even a bump or a bruise.

We also discovered that my car was now on the side of the road that we should have been traveling on (before we merged into oncoming traffic), facing the opposite direction. It was as if someone had simply picked us up like a matchbox car, and then plopped us back down in some dense grass on the side of the road. I remember people stopping to see if we were alright, and, surprisingly, the police were there in minutes. Someone had apparently called them right away.

After calling our parents and the tow truck, we all piled into the police car, and they dropped us off at a nearby gas station to wait for my parents to come pick us up. So, there we sat—at a plastic table in a gas station in the middle of the night, still shocked that we were all still alive. The older lady working at the register that night even took it upon herself to protect this group of stranded teenagers, reassuring us that she had a gun under the counter. We smiled as we considered the amount of God's protection we had all just experienced first-hand.

An evaluation of my car showed that the first accident of hitting the median had cracked the wheel axle which had eventually broken, leaving Chad with no control over the car. But an examination of the site of the accident was what left us entirely speechless. Although we drove that same road many more times after the accident, we could never again find that stretch of tall grass. The road is in Missouri, and it is known for its rock walls and steep drop-offs, not its grassy areas. But the Lord of Heaven's Armies created one for us that night. He rescued us by picking up a car, gently placing it in a grassy area that didn't exist, and saving four teenagers who ended up dedicating their lives to Him and to His work.

What about you?

Take some time to thank God for His provision in your life. Ask Him to show you ways He has provided for you that you might not have even known about.

Think of a specific time in your life when you know that God rescued you. Take time to share that story with someone today and bring Him glory.

Wowed by OUR FINANCIAL ADVISOR
by Lynne Biddle

"Teach those who are rich not to trust in their money, which is so unreliable. Their trust should be in God, who richly gives us all we need for our enjoyment." 1 Timothy 6:17 (NLT)

My husband and I had been married for about nine months and were living in married-student housing at Purdue University. We were the typical Ramen-Noodle eating, broke college students, except we were expecting our first child and had medical expenses to boot. On Sunday mornings we would drive into Lafayette, Indiana to worship at a wonderful, mission-oriented church.

One particular Sunday, after a visiting missionary presented his vision to the congregation, I felt very prompted by the Holy Spirit that we were to give one hundred dollars in the offering. One hundred dollars? That may as well have been one thousand or ten thousand on our measly budget. The money was just not there, and it was just not possible. As I tried to reason that prompting away, His voice in my spirit continued to persist: "Give one hundred dollars."

I looked at my husband, who seemed to be squirming in his seat. I whispered, "I feel like we are supposed to give one hundred dollars." His eyes got wide, and he said, "Me, too." So, I pulled out the checkbook, and with butterflies in my stomach, I remember praying, "God, please help us with this." The offering basket was passed, and with trepidation, the check went in.

The following day, nothing unusual happened, except that I was wondering if we were going to be able to eat that week. On Tuesday, when I returned home from my job, I went to the mailbox, and we had received an envelope from our insurance company. What could the insurance company be sending us? You guessed it. It was a check. But it was not a check for one hundred dollars. It was a check for more than three hundred dollars. The corresponding letter said that they had previously billed us for a wrong policy and that the enclosed check was a return of the difference.

ONE HUNDRED DOLLARS? THAT MAY AS WELL HAVE BEEN ONE THOUSAND.

We hadn't known that we had been wrongly billed. Nor did we know on that previous Sunday that money was coming our direction. But God knew. And isn't it just like God to intentionally set that money aside so that it could be a blessing to a missionary? And isn't it just like God to not only bless the missionary, but bless us as well? God's gift to us of the extra money in our budget that week was so helpful and appreciated. Looking back, however, I see that to us, the biggest blessing of this experience was the increasing of our faith in God as the most trustworthy financial advisor we will ever have.

What about you?

Is there something right now that God is prompting you to do or to give that you've been hesitant about? If so, I challenge you to step out in obedience and trust God with the outcome.

If not, I challenge you to continue to seek the Lord and tell Him you are available to be used however, whenever, and for whatever. That prayer, prayed sincerely, will rock your world.

Wowed by HIS DAILY PRESENCE
by Lois Knettle

"You will seek me and find me when you seek me with all your heart." Jeremiah 29:13 (NIV)

"And He walks with me and He talks with me, and He tells me I am His own." As a teenager, the chorus of this song meant so much to me because I knew I needed a firm foundation—to know and believe that I was indeed His. However, in my life, it wasn't until I was thirty-one years old that I first heard about receiving more of the Holy Spirit.

I learned that He wants to give daily help, insight, and direction to me—in very practical ways. The one thing that has most helped me in receiving more of Him is that as I awaken each morning, I verbally invite the Holy Spirit's presence and activity in me that day. How amazingly wonderful this is because I daily remind myself that He will come and be with me. This daily invitation has impacted me so greatly that now, forty-eight years later, this truth about His desire to be daily present is the most profound help I can share with anyone reading my story.

Two weeks ago, my husband and I had the privilege of taking a road trip to Mount Rushmore, Custer State Park, and Yellowstone National Park. Oh my, such incredible beauty we saw in God's marvelous creation! Each mile of the over four thousand that we drove was thrilling to us. After being on the road for eighteen days, we were quite tired as we neared the last leg of our trip back to our home in Michigan.

It was beginning to get dark, and we began to notice many deer along the woods beside the highway. Of course, this added some extra stress to my husband as he drove the remaining two hours of our trip. We both began to pray for safety. The last word of my prayer tumbled off my lips, specifically asking for safety for the deer, our truck and camper, and for ourselves. No sooner had I uttered those words than we suddenly saw something in the road up ahead of us. As we approached, we realized there was indeed a deer right in the middle of the road with two others standing along the side, waiting to cross.

Although that could have been a fatal accident for the deer or for us, God was watching over us, and He gave my husband the strength and awareness to see the deer in time and avoid any collision. Everything we asked for in prayer was covered, and we safely passed

WE BOTH BEGAN TO PRAY FOR SAFETY.

through that stretch of the road, arriving home with thankful hearts.

Being now in the almost seventy-ninth year of my life, there are so many, many times that the Holy Spirit has gently and tenderly spoken to give me direction, counsel, or guidance in a specific area of my life that I have raised up in prayer. What overwhelming joy overtakes us when we understand that He hears our prayers and answers in such perfect ways, according to our need. How I praise Him for these precious moments!

Yet, it is crucial that we take the time to ask, wait for His answer, and then act according to what we hear Him tell us. This is how we become more like Jesus. God always has more to give us of the Holy Spirit. Keep on asking daily for more, and He will continuously keep filling us, again and again, with His daily presence.

HOW I PRAISE HIM FOR THESE PRECIOUS MOMENTS!

What about you?

Do you invite more of the Holy Spirit's presence each day? If not, I strongly encourage you to begin.

Are you willing to wait, if necessary, for Him to speak, and then act on what you hear? Take time right now to wait upon Him and listen for His voice.

WOWED by GOD IN WHOM I TRUST
by Kristine Rusch

"Trust in the Lord with all your heart, and do not lean on your own understanding. In all your ways acknowledge him, and he will make straight your paths."
Proverbs 3:5-6 (ESV)

Back in the day when my husband, Patrick, and I were dating, he told me that he didn't play sports due to a heart condition that he had dealt with since he was little. I thought it was a heart murmur, and to me that was not a big deal. But, I found out it was a little more serious when he told me the story of when he was a kid and overheard his mom talking on the phone to their family doctor; Patrick heard her say that he would possibly not make it to his fifteenth birthday. What a scary thing to hear as a kid!

Thanks to the Lord, he had made it past what the doctors had predicted. We married in 1981, as he was nearing his twentieth birthday. Personally, I honestly didn't give much thought to his heart murmur anymore because it didn't seem like it was stopping him from doing what he wanted to do, and he didn't seem to be bothered by it either.

However, when we were living in Illinois, we went on a date night and headed out to our favorite buffet for dinner. While he was driving, something strange happened. His vision started to "close in and go dark," and he was afraid to drive. It was pouring down rain, so we pulled under an overpass and switched places and continued to head to the restaurant. As I was driving, he said his arms felt heavy and that I might want to head to the hospital. To shorten this story, he ended up having a heart catheterization, and they found that he may have had some calcium build up that broke away, which led to that weird vision sensation. So, we began to change a few things in our diet, and life went on.

Now, let me fast forward to the fall of 2014. In September, we had gone to Israel and upon our return to the States, Patrick seemed to get tired more easily. We weren't sure what was going on, and we somewhat brushed it off. In December our youngest daughter got married, we enjoyed Christmas, and we were ready to kick off a new year!

HE WAS AFRAID TO DRIVE.

But, in January 2015, my dad passed away unexpectedly, and it seemed as though Patrick was slowing down even more. It was normal for him to head to bed by 7:00 at night. Concerned, we went to his cardiologist who said he needed to have open heart surgery to replace his aortic valve. The doctor thought Patrick would be able to wait until November to have the surgery, but quickly changed his mind as it seemed he was "going downhill" at a faster pace than we thought.

His surgery was scheduled for April 15, 2015. My mind was going bonkers during all of this time as my mom had passed away in 2010, my middle brother in 2014, my dad in 2015, and now I was to face yet another hospital visit. It was really scary to me. I truly didn't want to lose Patrick too. I fasted and prayed for his surgery, and every time I prayed it seemed my thoughts went on and on: *What would I do if he passed? Would I stay in Midland? Would I stay in our house? Would I move? What would that mean for our kids?* So, I asked the Lord, "Why am I thinking like this? Are you trying to prepare me for his passing, or is the devil attacking me? I'm really not sure why I'm thinking this way!"

Then the Lord said to me, "Does it matter? Does it matter if he passes? Does it matter if he lives? Either way, you need to trust ME." It was right then and there that I told the Lord if He would take my hand and walk with me every step of the way, I would trust Him. I would know that if Patrick passed away, the Lord would still be at my side. And if Patrick pulled

WHAT WOULD I DO IF HE PASSED?

through surgery, He was still at my side and would bring Patrick through His healing. God "wowed" both of us as He brought both of us through that surgery with an amazing recovery and incredible story of His physical, emotional, and spiritual healing.

What about you?

Think about a time when you needed to trust God. What was it about, and how did you respond?

Take time to do a word study on the word "trust," and then personalize Proverbs 3:5-6 for your situation.

Wowed by THE GUILT TAKER
by Traci Presson

"'For I know the plans I have for you,' declares the Lord, 'plans to prosper you and not to harm you, plans to give you hope and a future.'" Jeremiah 29:11 (NIV)

October 16, 1995 and December 13, 1996—on one of these dates, it felt like everything was TAKEN, and on the other, like everything was GIVEN.

On October 16, 1995, I experienced a tubal pregnancy. Up until that time, I wasn't really interested in having kids. We had been married almost eight years, and a baby just wasn't our focus. But somehow the guilt, I will call it, of having that tubal pregnancy changed the course of my thinking. I am sure many reading this have experienced that "guilt" I am talking about, that feeling of losing a child.

Even though there was nothing that I could have done differently, when I saw the paperwork, I saw that it had been categorized as an "abortion." It was almost like I was a disgrace for something I had no control over. I remember thinking, *I didn't have an abortion. I had a tubal pregnancy.* But nevertheless, the hospitals wording was the same. I remember feeling such a heavy weight—a weight that should not be carried.

Fast forward to December 13, 1996. On that day, I gave birth to a sweet boy who even as I write this, is preaching in the background. I sit with tears running down my face at the faithfulness of God. You see, even in the midst of the pain that felt too heavy to carry four-teen months earlier (and left me with a small chance of future pregnancy), God

> **I REMEMBER FEELING SUCH A HEAVY WEIGHT— A WEIGHT THAT SHOULD NOT BE CARRIED.**

abundantly showered His grace, love, and mercy on me with a little bundle of joy.

God truly will never let you down, ever. Even when it appears everything around you is full of darkness and that nothing is going in the right direction, He is still walking patiently beside you. He is waiting on you to fully trust His plan for your life, which subsequently happens to be only for your good. Jeremiah 29:11 is a very familiar verse that reminds us of God's plans to prosper us and give us hope and a future. And that is exactly what He has done for me.

You may be feeling "heavy" for many reasons, some of which you had no control over, but some you feel are a direct result of something you did. Either way, the Father God wants to shower you with love. He longs to spend time with you. He is patiently waiting for you to bring Him what you need. So why don't you? He already knows anyway. He won't be taken by surprise at where you are in life or what you are thinking. Remember He has walked with you even when you haven't noticed Him there. God may do things differently than you wish they would have been done, but HE IS FAITHFUL.

What about you?

Write down a memory of something that you know you had no control over, but you still feel guilt over the outcome. Also write down a situation that you know happened as a direct result of something you did. Then lay that paper aside.

Read the following Scriptures out loud:

"Come to Me, all you who labor and are heavy laden, and I will give you rest." Matthew 11:28-30 (NKJV)

"Casting all your care upon Him, for He cares for you." I Peter 5:7 (NKJV)

"Fear not, for I am with you; be not dismayed, for I am your God. I will strengthen you, Yes, I will help you, I will uphold you with My righteous right hand." Isaiah 41:10 (NKJV)

Now, give the things on that paper over to the Lord Jesus, and then physically throw it in the trash. Rest in knowing you're loved and cherished by God. Every time you feel yourself picking that guilt back up, throw it away again. Allow Jesus to release you from that baggage.

THE ONE IN THE FUTURE
by Karen Prevost

"She is clothed with strength and dignity; she can laugh at the days to come."
Proverbs 31:25 (NIV)

It was Sunday, March 8, 2020, International Women's Day, celebrated with a huge parade in Madrid, Spain. Being a day to celebrate women, it seemed fitting to be reading Proverbs 31 that morning, the tribute to the virtuous woman. There was one verse in particular from that passage that the Lord used to tickle my curiosity—Proverbs 31:25.

How interesting! She can laugh at the future, even though she doesn't have a clue what's in store for her. How is that possible? Usually the future can fill us with fears or doubts because we are apprehensive about what might happen: a car accident, a serious illness, the loss of a job.

How was this woman of noble character able to laugh at the days to come? Then the Lord showed me how. It was because she knew who was in the future. God Himself was there. So she had no need to fear because she knew the Lord would be walking with her no matter what happened. It not only gave her peace, but filled her with laughter!

No sooner than I realized this, I had to put that verse to the test. Within one week, all of Spain was put under strict lockdown because of the rapidly spreading coronavirus. We were only allowed to leave our homes to buy groceries, go to the bank, or go to the pharmacy. And we had to go alone. We weren't even allowed to go for walks. As the quarantine continued to extend, we were confined to our homes for three months.

Could I laugh at the future during those days? The times I took a step back from the news broadcasts and social media and set my eyes on eternity, I could see the light of God's greater purpose at the end of the tunnel. Other days the fears of an unknown and unfriendly future for my children and grandchildren smothered hope and stole sleep. But as time slowed down, I learned to seek the Lord in deeper ways, to listen to His heart, and to reach out to others. Nearly every morning the Lord put someone on my heart to connect with, and time after time, I saw Him touch people in unexpected ways. Some of the greatest treasures were reconnecting with people I hadn't been in contact with for years—college

COULD I LAUGH AT THE FUTURE DURING THOSE DAYS?

classmates, distant relatives, old friends.

One of these treasures was a woman we had ministered to thirty years ago when she was just a teenager in our church in southern Spain. She happened to post a random comment on a Facebook post I made at the beginning of the quarantine. We began to text, then do video calls. Within days, Toñi had recommitted her life to Jesus. We prayed together and studied the Bible together virtually, and I was able to put her in touch with a local church in her area. That whole experience brought me so much joy! God was in the details. He had been waiting for me in the future.

No matter how chaotic the world grows with threats of the worldwide pandemic, economic collapse, volatile politics, and racial unrest, I know Jesus is waiting for me in the future. No matter how dire the future may look, I know God will walk with me there. His presence is what I need. All of my hope is in Him. As David wrote in Psalm 16:11, ". . . in your presence there is fullness of joy" (ESV). I can laugh at the days to come.

What about you?

What are some concerns you have about your future?

Imagine Jesus waiting for you in the future. How does He change how you see it?

Spend some time thanking Him for how He will walk with you in every situation you ever face.

Wowed by SWOLLEN ANKLES AND FEET
by Wendy Elarton

"But I have been pouring out my soul before the Lord. Do not regard your servant as a worthless woman, for all along I have been speaking out of my great anxiety and vexation." 1 Samuel 1:15b-16 (ESV)

Opening my old journals, I sometimes find things I placed in them to remind me of special memories. I have a homemade Mother's Day card in this one. Thoughts are flooding my heart as I recall a time when I could totally relate to Hannah in the Bible. Struggling with her inability to have a child, she says the Scripture above to Eli the priest.

Our journey to have a child was like many who struggle with infertility. Disappointment met us every month, and we experienced feelings of loss. I spent hours pouring my soul out to the Lord as questions filled my mind: *What do we need to do? Why was the Lord taking us through such heart-breaking disappointment? Could He not see how faithful we were to Him and totally dedicated to His Church?*

We met with a fertility doctor only to find out that getting pregnant would not be easy for us. We began the process of expensive medicine and everything in our power to have a baby. Thinking back to those days, I remember begging God for a healing and feeling like I was, as Hannah put it, "a worthless woman."

Finally, one day my prayer was answered—a daughter was on the way! Someone blessed us with a pink rocking chair, and I would sit and rock in it with great excitement. My body was huge, and sitting felt so good to relieve the swollen ankles and feet. I could only see my feet when I sat down. Despite the misery of my body, knowing we had made it to the last trimester (and I would soon be holding a baby girl in that rocking chair) made the chair even more comfortable.

Freedom from those swollen ankles and feet finally came with a 9-pound, 2-ounce baby girl—Abigail Lea. What a miracle. I was so amazed that I was actually a mother. The sacrifices of money and physical challenges were so worth it all. Motherhood was even better than what women had bragged to me about.

I was happy with our tiny family, but as we began our church plant, I realized how lonely it could be for our baby, Abby. I made an appointment to see the fertility doctor again. One more child would be nice, and I thought we could sacrifice again for such a wonderful gain. Still, knowing the months of trials and sacrifices (and even the humility involved in people knowing our struggles) brought me back to another prayer: *God couldn't you just heal me? We are sacrificing everything for you to build your church in this new community.*

This prayer was still on my heart when we took our small church family (twenty people) to a revival service in Grand Rapids. At the end of the service, a call was made to come forward for prayer for healing. I decided my example of moving forward into the aisle would encourage our group. Many laid their hands on me and asked for a healing touch. Feeling so thankful for their support, we traveled home.

A few days later we visited the same fertility doctor, knowing she knew our circumstances, and we asked to try again. A prescription was filled, and we began the first month. To our surprise, we were pregnant the very next month! Rounding the corner of the last trimester again with swollen ankles and feet, my relief finally came after giving birth to a 9-pound, 8-ounce baby boy, Gabriel Lynn. I was very grateful and content with the blessings God had given us. I was again wowed by the goodness of the Lord.

Being a busy mom with two little ones, and Nathan busy with work and church, the months went by fast. Never in my wildest dreams did I ever think that we would be expecting another baby. In fact, when I found out I was pregnant just ten months after delivering Gabriel, it took me by surprise; I felt very unready, and I was not longing for swollen ankles and feet again at all.

My mind and my heart waged a little bit of an internal war about how I could feel this way. I came to the realization that God had answered my prayer and healed me before, and He wanted to show me what He had done. My third baby, Levi Nathan, weighed in at 9 pounds, 10 ounces. Wow. God knew we needed baby number three and what he would bring to our family.

So, as I open this old journal again and see my precious homemade Mother's Day card, I can't help but smile. I am so thankful for His miraculous healing touch and answered prayers—even if it meant quite a few months of swollen ankles and feet.

What about you?

Have you been in a place where you thought God could not hear your great cry? Have you asked and asked until you feel like He doesn't care?

Take time today to say, "God I recognize that I may be disappointed in You for not answering my prayer." Then, begin to read and think about Isaiah 55:8-9.

Wowed by HIS PROVISION
by Karen Grabill

"I was young and now I am old; yet I have not seen the righteous forsaken or their children begging bread." Psalms 37:25 (KJV)

As with King David of old, I can say from life experience that this verse is absolutely true. In what seems like a lifetime ago, my husband, Dean, was a first-year student at Gordon Divinity School pursuing a Master of Divinity degree. We were newly married, had relocated from our home state in Pennsylvania to Massachusetts, and were serving as part-time youth pastors at a church in the Boston suburbs.

We had to live very frugally since attending seminary full-time was costly, and our various jobs were barely meeting our needs. It was a tremendous lesson to learn early in our marriage that God truly does keep His promises and care for His children. We were renting a second-floor furnished apartment above a local bookstore in the quaint little town of Beverly Farms. It was a beautiful setting, and we felt very blessed.

One Friday evening, we travelled south to our church to take our youth to a special rally. We thought nothing of leaving our two quarters and three dimes on our bedroom dresser so that the following day I could go to the laundromat to do our two loads of laundry for the week. We took our remaining few dollars with us in case the youth wanted to stop for a snack after the youth service. We did, in fact, spend our last dollar on the way home.

When we arrived back at our apartment, we noticed that our entryway door didn't look right, and as we went up the steps to our private door, the lock was broken and the door was ajar. This was unnerving, to say the least. Then, we entered the apartment and found that it was slightly askew. But, when we walked into the bedroom, it was a disaster. We could tell that it had been gone through hurriedly but thoroughly. The closet was a mess, and the dresser drawers had been opened and searched. Things on top of the dresser had been moved, but to our amazement, there still lay the two quarters and three dimes for our laundry!

When the police came and we checked our possessions, we realized that NOTHING of ours had been stolen. (We evidently didn't have anything of value!) The thieves did take money from the bookstore downstairs, but they left us our eighty cents.

THIS WAS UNNERVING TO SAY THE LEAST.

Of course, any break-in does make one feel threatened and vulnerable, but it could have been so much worse. The Lord had everything under control. We weren't home, and it was a blessing to be poor! Best of all, we learned that God cares for His children, and even in difficult circumstances, He provides for their needs—even if it is just for clean laundry.

What about you?

Think about a time God came through for you with a provision for a real need. How did that make you feel? Give Him praise right now for His abundant blessings in your life.

If God did it before, do you believe He is still concerned about you today?

WOWED by THE GOD OF COMPASSION
by Jennie Singer

"And he passed in front of Moses, proclaiming, 'The LORD, the LORD, the compassionate and gracious God, slow to anger, abounding in love and faithfulness, maintaining love to thousands, and forgiving wickedness, rebellion and sin.'" Exodus 34:6-7 (NIV)

The Lord's description of Himself in Exodus 34:6-7 is repeated numerous times throughout the remainder of the Bible. The first adjective that He uses to describe Himself is "compassionate," which is translated from the Hebrew word "rakhum." One of the writers for the Bible Project points out that this noun is closely related to the Hebrew word for womb—"rekhem," painting a picture of the way the Lord is moved out of His character to care for His people as a mother cares for her child. This is how I felt the Lord and His people cared for me and my husband after we miscarried our first child.

My husband Jake and I were elated when we discovered we were pregnant. We started searching for a care provider and soon told our families, who were equally (if not more) excited. We had been praying for a child and were so thankful for His miracle of life!

However, around seven or eight weeks into the pregnancy I started to feel less nauseous and averse to smells, which caused me to worry and to pray because everything I read said that improvements of that sort normally begin after the first trimester. I asked the Lord to give me some sort of reassurance that the baby was healthy, but I did not hear anything like that from Him.

About three weeks after we shared the news with our families, we were told during a trip to the hospital that the baby had stopped growing a month prior, and we were going to lose him or her. We were shocked and heartbroken. We left and tried to prepare for whatever was going to happen next.

Twenty-nine hours later, in the middle of the night, we returned to the hospital because the on-and-off pain I was experiencing turned into constant, excruciating pain. Jake helped check me in, and we were quickly taken to a room where we met two kind nurses. I asked for pain medication, and they informed me that I would have to wait to see a doctor before they administered any drugs.

WE WERE SHOCKED AND HEARTBROKEN.

Their calm explanation was quickly met with my rude response, "Are you kidding me?" Yet, they continued to be gentle and caring towards me (despite my bad temper). I remember the younger nurse's face showed concern, while the more experienced nurse had an expression of empathy and sorrow as I endured both the physical and emotional pain. She comforted me until the physical pain subsided.

The doctor finally arrived and told us that my body was ready to begin healing. Jake and I left feeling sorrowful and downcast, but the Lord used the following weeks to teach us to experience His joy during suffering. We tasted the sweetness of His presence. His Holy Spirit ministered to me through the emergency room nurses, our families, and through Jake—the most loving husband.

Many members of our church family also showed His compassion through persistent prayer, providing meals and help around the house, and through encouraging words. Colossians 3:12 says, "Therefore, as God's chosen people, holy and dearly loved, clothe yourselves with compassion, kindness, humility, gentleness and patience" (NIV). I learned from each person what it looks like to be "clothed in compassion."

Although our expectations of growing our earthly family weren't met at that time, we soon found peace knowing that our child now rejoices in the glorious presence of Jesus. The love and care I felt for the child who was in my womb for a short time is incomparable to the love and compassion the Father has for His children—those who are forever held in His "rekhem."

What about you?

Recall a time when you experienced God's compassion towards you, His caring for you as a mother cares for her child. Share that story with a friend or family member.

Have you ever experienced His joy through suffering? How?

"The Lord directs the steps of the godly. He delights in every detail of their lives." Psalms 37:23 (NLT)

Years ago, my friend and I really felt challenged to be obedient to God and to share the gospel with those around us. We had heard messages about being disciples and trusting God to lead us. We began to pray and ask God for divine appointments.

After one of these times of praying, we felt led to go camping at a very popular campground on a holiday weekend. People usually book months in advance for these spots, but we felt like God would give us one. When we showed up, there was one spot open. As we began to set up camp, we realized the zipper on our tent was broken. We laughed and went to our camp neighbors to ask for some duct tape.

As we chatted, we realized that we were camping in the middle of a huge family reunion, and the people in all the sites surrounding us were related. We then heard that just before we arrived, two members of their family (who were on their way to the campground) had been in a bad **THERE WAS ONE SPOT OPEN.** car accident, and one of them was in critical condition. It was their spot we were camping in. We felt led to begin praying with our camp neighbors for this couple whom we didn't even know.

The family began coming over every few hours and giving us updates. Things were not looking good, and parts of the man's body were shutting down. We felt led to pray as we got each update for those specific parts, and they began to function again! There was a miracle happening in this man's body and within his family.

Needless to say, this man and his wife survived the accident. We ministered to this man's family throughout the weekend and shared the hope we have in Christ. Later, we were invited to share this story with his church and other churches in his town. Our God is the God of miracles. He led us to exactly where He wanted us to be so we could bring the gospel, encouragement, and hope in a time of despair. He led my friend and me to start asking for divine appointments in our everyday life. He taught us that all we have to do is listen and be obedient, and then go and say and do what He tells us. We are His vessels.

What about you?

Can you recall a "divine appointment" that God has set for you? If so, remember what He has done in the past and ask Him to do it again. If not, I encourage you to ask God to set one and to show you how He wants to use you.

1 Peter 3:15 says, "But in your hearts revere Christ as Lord. Always be prepared to give an answer to everyone who asks you to give the reason for the hope you have" (NIV). I feel challenged by the word "always" in this verse. Do people see hope in you? Do you share the reason for the hope you have?

Wowed by THE ONE IN THE BOAT WITH ME
by Anonymous

"He saw the disciples straining at the oars, because the wind was against them. Shortly before dawn he went out to them, walking on the lake. He was about to pass by them, but when they saw him walking on the lake, they thought he was a ghost. They cried out, because they all saw him and were terrified. Immediately he spoke to them and said, 'Take courage! It is I. Don't be afraid.' Then he climbed into the boat with them, and the wind died down. They were completely amazed." Mark 6:48-51 (NIV)

Have you ever been asked to do something really hard or difficult? It's one thing to have the option to choose if you want to do that hard thing or not. It's totally different when you don't have a choice, and you find yourself straining at the oars of life with strong winds against you. Parenting adult children can feel like that at times.

My husband and I were enjoying our time together watching a football game. I remember the sun was shining, and it was a beautiful day. Our oldest daughter came through the back door with her best friend. She seemed anxious about something, like she had to say something difficult or tell us something she had already done. My husband recalls thinking she was going to tell us she'd joined the military or had made another big decision without seeking our advice beforehand.

> **IT'S ONE THING TO HAVE THE OPTION TO CHOOSE IF YOU WANT TO DO THAT HARD THING OR NOT.**

Then, she finally found the courage to say, "I have to tell you something. I'm afraid to tell you because I'm afraid you'll be very disappointed. That's why I brought my friend with me." I immediately knew what she was going to tell us. So, I asked, "Are you pregnant?" It was as if her whole body relaxed because she didn't have to actually say those words.

This was our opportunity, as parents, to love our daughter with the love of Jesus regardless of the sinful act, to accept her for who she was in that moment, and to make a difference in this situation that we now found ourselves in. We told her we loved her in spite of what she had done, that we would love her throughout the entire process, and that we would love her baby through it all.

Our daughter was only nineteen years old at the time, and she herself would admit this process made her grow up quickly. Today she is an amazing wife and mother of three beautiful and wonderful children. She has been through many ups and downs, but she has remained steadfast and strong. I believe it's because of the love of Christ we displayed during those initial moments.

There have been many other difficult times in our years of parenting, and with each difficult circumstance, I've had times of questioning my parenting abilities. I've had many moments to reflect on the questions of *Where did I go wrong? or What could I have done differently? or How did I fail in raising them to walk with the Lord?*

Although I still have regrets for my mistakes every once in a while, I choose to remind myself of what the song "O Come to the Altar" says: *"Leave behind your regrets and mistakes. Come today there's no reason to wait. Jesus is calling. Bring your sorrows and trade them for joy. From the ashes a new life is born."*

I've had to learn how to trust, follow, give grace (to others and to myself), and love with the love of Christ. Most of all, I've learned to take every thought captive and take it to the Lord. No, I'm not a perfect parent, but I do know the power of prayer. It's what gets me through every day, and it's what reminds me that I don't strain at those oars on my own. Jesus is in the boat with me, and He still has the power to calm the wind and the waves.

What about you?

When you walk through a difficult time in your life, how do you most often respond? Do you blame yourself or others, walk in fear, or remain at peace (knowing Who is in the boat with you)?

Is there a past mistake for which you've been unable to accept His forgiveness? Take some time to pray, and to receive His mercy and grace.

Wowed by THE GOD WHO LOVES ME AS I AM
by Kelly Rhoads

"This Good News tells us how God makes us right in his sight. This is accomplished from start to finish by faith. As the Scriptures say, 'It is though faith that a righteous person has life.'" Romans 1:17 (NLT)

Most of us raised in the church grew up singing the song "Jesus Loves Me." After hearing it for a lifetime, we can become desensitized to this great truth. Jesus loves me, just as I am. After many years of looking first at myself—instead of looking at Jesus— and not seeing myself through His eyes, the revelation of His perfect love has captured my heart and mind once more. I am now living life a whole new way in freedom and in truth.

I was saved and baptized at a young age. I believed in God, but I had a child's understanding of Him. At eighteen, I had an encounter with Jesus that forever changed me, and I truly surrendered my life to Him. In Luke 9:23, Jesus says to the crowd, "If any of you wants to be my follower, you must turn from your self-

> **WE CAN BECOME DESENSITIZED TO THIS GREAT TRUTH.**

ish ways, take up your cross daily and follow me" (NLT). After my transforming experience with Him, I started absorbing the Word of God, and I felt I finally started understanding what it meant—like this love letter was intimately written to me. I could finally understand the message, and I wanted to please my Father.

After getting married, my husband and I moved four times, which meant we had four different church-life experiences. Plus, I'm an avid reader and love many Christian authors. I spent many years hearing and reading about how I could be a better Christian if I would just do more, give more, be more, change more, help more, and the list goes on and on. I felt I was always running behind the "Christian elite," and I was never quite measuring up. I constantly saw myself missing the mark of perfection. I became so legalistic in my thinking that I lost my freedom in Jesus and became entangled in the lie that I was "not good enough."

My life changed several years ago when my sister told me about a preacher she was listening to that was helping to transform her love of God. I started listening to him, and it was as if heavy weights were coming off my heart and mind. I finally received the truth: Jesus loves me—just as I am—not because of what I do. It was as if the years of lies I believed about myself were finally brought to light. My mind and heart connected and bonded to the truth. Romans 8:15 says, "So you have not received a spirit that makes you fearful slaves. Instead, you received God's Spirit when he adopted you as his own children" (NLT).

Jesus loves me as a Father, and His love is so overwhelmingly beautiful. He's my protector, my provider, my guide, my help, my friend, and so much more. Everything He asks of me to do or not to do is influenced by His love and care of me and is for my best. Every mention of Jesus in a sermon, in a song, or through the Word has made me so emotionally connected and tender, understanding how much He truly loves me.

Again, just like when I was eighteen, I have fallen in love with the Word of God. It literally feeds my starving soul.

What about you?

Have you ever struggled with trying to hit the mark of perfection and feeling like you're not enough? If so, remind yourself of Romans 8:1: "So now there is no condemnation for those who belong to Christ Jesus" (NLT). God's word tells us that we are saved by His grace, not by our "perfect" works. Praise God for His incredible grace and love!

The Word of God is actually a love letter from God to you! Take a moment and write this "gift tag" somewhere on the first few pages of your Bible: To: (your name), From: Your Heavenly Father. Then spend some moments thanking Him for such an extravagant gift.

Wowed by THE ONE WHO ERASES BUMPS
by Linda Chastain

"He pleaded earnestly with him, 'My little daughter is dying. Please come and put your hands on her so that she will be healed and live.'" Mark 5:23 (NIV)

When our daughter was five years old, we noticed she had a growth on her shin bone. It wasn't bothering her or sensitive to touch. There was no bruise or scratch. I made an appointment with her pediatrician, but he wasn't sure what it was. So, he referred us to a pediatric surgeon for further examination. A CT scan was done on her leg, and the results indicated to him that the growth on her shin bone was cancerous. He advised surgery to remove the lump ASAP.

Our hearts sank as we processed the news. The side effect of this operation would be that the cancerous leg would always be shorter than the healthy one, so our daughter would always walk with a limp. The cancer cells were in close proximity to her growth plate, so their removal would affect the normal growth of that leg.

HE ADVISED SURGERY TO REMOVE THE LUMP ASAP.

My husband and I did not feel comfortable moving forward with this procedure without going to prayer first. We prayed, asked fellow believers to pray, and took our little girl to the altar at church where she was anointed and prayed over. As we presented our daughter's need at a prayer meeting, a woman came and knelt beside me and laid her hands on me. I felt as if she lifted me to His throne room with her, and I knew that this prayer warrior had spent much time there.

In the next few days, I noticed that the growth on her leg was decreasing! I was amazed by the mighty work God was doing. Soon afterwards, we had an appointment for another CT scan and another meeting with the surgeon. He showed us the old scan (with visible growth and many extra cells), and then he placed the new scan beside it to compare the two. The new scan showed no growth and no extra cell activity at all. My daughter's shin was totally flat.

The doctor was flabbergasted, and he had no explanation. We told him about how many people had been praying for her, but he just stopped us and said there was no possible reason this could have happened. It was obvious he felt very uncomfortable, and he left quickly and never returned. Needless to say, we left rejoicing and telling everyone we could about how God had performed a miracle and healed our little girl! Wow. What a loving Father we serve.

What about you?

Do you know people who will not acknowledge God's existence and supernatural work?

Use the next few minutes to pray for them, that their eyes and hearts will be opened to the truth.

Wowed by PRAYING WHILE MOWING
by Karen Hlavin

"Show Your marvelous lovingkindness by Your right hand, O You who save those who trust in You from those who rise up against them. Keep me as the apple of Your eye; hide me under the shadow of Your wings." Psalms 17:7-8 (NKJV)

It was a beautiful summer day, and my husband, Jeff, was in the back yard mowing the lawn. He often would pray as he walked back and forth.

That was the case this day. As he was enjoying his time with the Lord, he suddenly had a very strong feeling of urgency to pray for our son. It was the kind of "weighty" thing that caused him to feel that Aaron was in great danger. He prayed earnestly in the Spirit for approximately three minutes, and then just as suddenly, the burden lifted.

When Jeff was finished, he came in the house and told me about the unusual thing that had happened, and we both wondered what it could mean. A few minutes later, Aaron came bursting through the door, out of breath and with big eyes. "Dad! Mom! You won't believe what just happened! While I was over at David's house, we were riding his go-kart out in the street." (David lived on a cul-de-sac with six houses.) "I decided to go out onto the main street. There was a car parked right at the corner, and when I pulled onto the main street, I was right in front of a car coming straight at me. I didn't see him, and he did not see me until we were face-to-face. Dad, I was so scared! He just missed me by an inch!" We quickly shared with Aaron what had happened regarding Jeff's strong need to pray just moments before.

Our son could have died or been seriously injured that day. But God had other plans. The cool thing about it is that He included my husband in those plans. Aaron learned about God's loving protection and how God uses our prayers for one another. It wasn't just a lesson for **"HE JUST MISSED ME BY AN INCH!"** Aaron; it was also a faith lesson for both Jeff and me. I never stop being amazed by God's love and care for us!

I've learned a couple things that have served me well through the years. When I feel God's prompting to stop what I'm doing and pray, I need to pay attention. Sometimes we find out why, and sometimes we never know why we have prayed for someone.

I want to continue to develop and keep that sensitivity to His promptings. I also realize that even when I can't be there with our children and grandchildren to watch over them, God is always there. He is with them, and He loves them even more than I do.

Has everything always gone perfectly for my family? No. Have they ever been hurt? Yes, but I have always trusted God even in those moments. I can get in the way if I don't trust. I have also learned that sometimes, when things don't go smoothly for my kids or even for Jeff and me, God is maturing and growing us into the people He wants us to be.

I CAN GET IN THE WAY IF I DON'T TRUST.

What about you?

Have you ever sensed God's prompting to stop what you're doing and pray? Did you pay attention?

How have you "got in the way" by not trusting God in certain difficult moments? What have you learned?

Wowed by GOD'S PERFECT TIMING
by Kyja Malone

**"But I trust in you, LORD; I say, 'You are my God.' My times are in your hands."
Psalms 31:14-15a (NIV)**

I'd like to take you on a journey. My husband, Michael, and I had begun to pray about where to send our daughter to kindergarten the following year. She is our first-born, and we felt the weight of this decision. We were considering sending Lily to one of the Christian schools in town. A big concern was how we were going to pay for it. Little did we know, although there were some bends in the road ahead, God was already mapping out the perfect route:

March 2, 2019 (journal entry)
I want to circle in prayer the decision of where to send Lily to school next year. In the grand scheme of things, the decision of where to send her to school seems small, but I know that nothing is too big or too small for God.

March 16, 2019 (journal entry)
I found out yesterday that my job will not be renewed next year. God, I don't know what you have in store for me and our family, but I am excited to see what You do. Help me to trust in You, and know that even though things feel scary and uncertain, You have a plan—a great plan. You know exactly what is coming next, and it's good.

April 2019
We continue to pray about where to send Lily to school. On top of losing my job, we are expecting to have our third baby in August. More and more, God is leading us towards this private Christian school, but what would have required "tightening the belt" before, now seems impossible to pay for.

May 17, 2019 (journal entry, written during a prayer service at church)
Lord, I come tonight feeling overwhelmed, anxious, and scared about what to do for Lily next year. I am here to pray for wisdom and peace. The Lord led me to Ephesians 5:15, "Look carefully then how you walk, not as unwise but as wise, making the best use of the time, because the days are evil. Therefore, do not be foolish but understand what the will of the Lord is" (ESV). We make the decision that night to send Lily to the Christian school. God's peace immediately follows which confirms that we are on His path.

August 7, 2019

My husband is admitted to the hospital because of a tumor on his spine that would later be diagnosed as stage IV lymphoma.

August 9, 2019

I go into labor. Our beautiful baby girl arrives, and our hearts are filled with joy.

August 12, 2019

We receive the first bill for school, about $650, which we are able to pay. Our income has been drastically reduced. *What will six months of cancer treatments cost? How long until our new baby's hospital bills come? Should we still send Lily to a private school that costs so much?* At this moment, we take the time to pray and decide to trust that God knew what He was doing when He led us to choose this school months before. We made that first tuition payment.

August 14, 2019

We receive the most amazing email from Lily's school. It reads: "There was an anonymous gift for your tuition! The tuition for the REST OF THE YEAR has been completely paid…" Many tears of joy are shed over reading this email. We cry and thank God for His faithfulness and goodness. The Lord used that anonymous gift of $2600 in tuition money to not only fill a huge need, but to give us faith.

As the journey of life had brought us another newborn baby to raise, the start of a school year, and the unknowns of cancer, He reminded us that He was there and that He saw us. Since God had so perfectly taken care of our financial needs, we knew we could trust Him to take care of our other needs as well. Only He knew what we needed, when we needed it. His timing is perfect in ALL things.

What about you?

Reflect on a time when you experienced God's perfect timing in your life. Then, thank Him for His wisdom and attention to every detail.

TROUBLE
by Linda Chastain

"I have told you these things, so that in me you may have peace. In this world you will have trouble. But take heart! I have overcome the world." John 16:33 (NIV)

I knew something different was going on in my body that month. My husband and I had experienced a miscarriage over three years ago, but not long after that, we started trying to have another baby. Even though we still felt loss and heartache, God had removed all anger and replaced it with loving acceptance as only He can do. Also, our seven-year-old daughter (who was herself a miracle baby) kept us busy. When I explained to the nurse at my doctor's office what my symptoms were, she made an appointment for me the next day.

An ultrasound was performed as well as a pregnancy test which made me excited! However, the doctor called soon afterwards to tell me that it appeared it was a tubal or ectopic pregnancy. My heart sank. Since it is very dangerous if the tube ruptures and immediate medical care is not available, the doctor told me to check into the hospital right away.

After admission to the hospital, I was confined to bed rest, and a daily ultrasound was performed. The results of the ultrasound remained the same—no fertilized egg was visible. I started allowing fear of the unknown to enter my thoughts, but I recognized the originator of those thoughts immediately. I cried out to my loving Savior to just wrap His arms around me because I needed to feel safe and secure, knowing He had control of the situation.

My doctor came into my hospital room and told me that since my ectopic pregnancy could not be proven through an ultrasound, he would have to discharge me the next day due to insurance limitations. But my doctor prayed with me that night, and we asked for God's guidance. God was still impressing upon him that I had a tubal pregnancy. He felt it could be too dangerous for me to be discharged, especially since we lived about forty minutes from the hospital.

I woke up the next morning not feeling well with some pain in my abdomen. As I laid in my hospital bed that afternoon, I prayed that this uncertainty would end. Then, that afternoon, I began experiencing pain which was so intense that I started hyperventilating. I felt like I was going to black out. I called out, "Help me God!" I distinctly felt His presence, and my breathing started slowing down.

The nurses quickly told me that my tube was starting to rupture, and I was rushed to the operating room. My doctor "just happened" to already be at the hospital with another patient. I knew that it was no accident that my doctor was available to do immediate surgery. My God had total control. I was able to speak to my Spirit-filled doctor in the operating room a minute before I was given anesthesia. Knowing my doctor would be guided by the hand of God brought me enormous relief and thankfulness.

When I woke up, I discovered that the surgery had been done just in time, and there was no major internal bleeding or organ damage. If I hadn't started feeling some pain early that morning, I would have been discharged, and my life easily could have been in danger. My loving heavenly Father was watching over me, orchestrating the rupturing to happen while I was still in the hospital close to emergency help.

After my discharge from the hospital, I arrived home—thankful that the nightmare was over but also physically and emotionally drained. Once I was home, I looked at our daughter with even more gratitude to God for the miracle of her life. As I had more time to process what had just happened, my grief began. In the last five years of trying to have another child, I had been pregnant twice and lost both. I didn't think I could deal with the loss of any more babies emotionally, physically, or mentally.

My husband and I both felt like we needed to pray to understand what God was telling us, and we asked Him to reveal His plan for our family, not ours. *Should we persevere and trust that we would get pregnant again? Or are You saying "No"?* Finally, after much prayer, we felt like God was saying, "No."

It's easy to say "Hallelujah" when He answers our prayers the way we want, but it's more difficult to say those words when we don't get our way. When we ask, we sometimes expect Him to just rubber stamp our preference. But, who are we to expect our plans to be better than the plans of the Creator, King, and Sovereign God who loves us unconditionally and knows the beginning to the end? Jesus tells us that in this world we will have trouble, but He has overcome the world. *God, You knew I was going to have an ectopic pregnancy, and Your hand of protection covered me every step of the way. I am amazed by You!*

What about you?

How do you normally respond when God doesn't answer your prayers in the way you'd like Him to? What "trouble" do you have in this world right now that you need to trust Him with?

Wowed by HIS HAND IN THE DARKNESS
by Anonymous

"And I will lead the blind in a way they do not know, in paths they have not known I will guide them. I will turn the darkness before them into light, the rough places into level ground. These are the things I do, and I do not forsake them." Isaiah 42:16 (ESV)

I'm a Bible study leader, and our last study tackled Isaiah. The year was a tough one for me, for sure. I was newly divorced and really struggling to parent my rebellious and hurting teenage son while continuing to be a constant for my less challenging (but no less important) other children. It'd been a tumultuous week when I sat down to read the week's study passage. I kept re-reading the same paragraph over and over, and then I would get distracted and pull away. I didn't read the full passage until the day before class met. When I did, this verse (Isaiah 42:16) took my breath away, and I just cried at God's goodness.

Now, it's a great verse all on its own, but God had laid some groundwork earlier that day to make it downright spectacular for me. I was at the coffeeshop where my son worked, and I always introduced myself to the baristas to get a sense of his co-workers. I was chatting with Nate-the-Barista, and as we were talking, he asked me if my son was anything like I had been as a teen (not a typical question). It struck me as an unusual question, but the answer was easy—a resounding no! I had been an ultra-obedient, very compliant kid, and I've NEVER tried most of the stuff my son is into. His view on the world, his desires, and his view on authority are all very foreign to me. I've definitely been very aware of how different he is from anything I've ever done or wanted to do. So, it was interesting question to be asked.

Fast forward to that evening when I was finally reading this verse. I was so moved by God's assertion that He leads the blind in a way that they do not know, in paths they have not known. (Have you ever felt totally clueless and helpless, blinded by your lack of orientation?) It's one thing to trust God to give us patience and faith as we raise kids who are like us, or to trust that God will get us safely home from work or from the store. We know those paths. It's another thing when God leads us into places we feel totally lost in and are utterly disoriented by—and He knows this and takes us through them, clearing a path through the obstacles for us.

I love that God not only gave me this promise, but He also took the time to give me that encounter with Nate-the-Barista which highlighted that I really, really don't know or understand the path I'm on, but HE does. He sees my fears. He sees my complete lack of experience with what I'm facing. All weekend I prayed with all my heart that God would help me to trust Him through this next season, even though I have no idea what it's going to look like. THIS was God answering that prayer. I really needed this assurance in the next few weeks as things with my son escalated to the point that he left my house. God's timing was perfect.

On top of that, not only did God answer my prayer for direction and faith, but as I told my Bible study group about this encounter, we discovered that Nate-the-Barista was the son of one of the ladies in my group. She'd been praying for her

HE SEES MY FEARS.

son to know Jesus in a real and meaningful way all year in her prayer requests. It was such a neat moment to see that God had used her son (for whom we'd been praying all year) to encourage me. It was yet another reminder of the ways that God carefully constructs our stories and answers our prayers in layers and timings that we can't imagine.

So, I'm praying this verse over each of you, too. I pray that you will feel God's right hand leading you through whatever darkness you are facing right now, that even if you are in a place you have never been before, you will KNOW that God is not surprised or at a loss, but that He is giving you light, guiding you, leveling obstacles, never forsaking you. Big things or small things—none of them are out of His care and ability.

What about you?

Reread the last paragraph and allow this prayer to wash over you. Lay aside any doubt, fear, or confusion and simply rest in His care, power, and ability to turn the darkness into light, the rough places into level ground.

Wowed by THE GOD WHO SAVES
by Pam Wellington

"This is good and pleases God our Savior, who wants everyone to be saved and to understand the truth." 1 Timothy 2:3-4 (NLT)

It was June of 2006, and my dad was in the hospital on the other side of the state. When I arrived, Dad had a horrible cough and was struggling to breathe, so I chose to stay with him rather than going to his house to sleep.

Early the next morning, a doctor arrived to share the results of the previous day's x-rays. After introducing himself, he quickly asked, "Did you know that your father has stage four lung cancer?" I was thunderstruck. None of us had any idea, although we had known that my father had been a former smoker decades ago.

I asked what kind of treatment the doctor would recommend. His next statement was even more astonishing: "None. It's too late for treatment of any kind. The cancer is far too advanced and has taken its toll. I expect that your father won't last more than a few days."

My father had been resting during this exchange with the doctor. Once he woke up, I broke the news to Dad as gently as I could. He took it in stride, seemingly not that surprised. It made me wonder if he had known, or at least suspected, this diagnosis.

My biggest fear in that moment was that my dad had yet to accept Christ as His Savior. I had been raised in a religious home with our family attending church every Sunday. But, at the age of twenty-nine, I exchanged my religion for a true relationship with my Savior. With my new-found zeal for the Lord, I told everyone what had happened to me, including my parents.

I vividly recall a day when they were visiting at my home, and I tried to share my faith once again. My father shook his finger in my face demanding, "Don't you EVER speak to me of these things again!" He then instructed my mother to get her coat because they were leaving, which they promptly did. Through the coming years, we saw each other fairly often, but I had not talked to him again about God.

Now here I was, alone with my dying father. I prayed, "God, in Your great mercy, give me an open door and my dad a softened heart." In the meantime, my father had a rough couple of days. Before my sister could arrive, he had fallen into a comatose state,

DON'T YOU EVER SPEAK TO ME OF THESE THINGS AGAIN!

still on oxygen, and only occasionally had drifted briefly back into consciousness. Mostly, he was out.

During the first three days, I spent the bulk of those hours praying and singing Christian songs over my father. Sleep was elusive, so my vigil continued into the night as well. My prayers were answered as God did two incredible miracles during those last days of my father's life.

While Dad had prepared a will, no papers for medical power of attorney had ever been signed by any of us kids. After being told about our dilemma, a friend arrived at the hospital with the necessary papers in hand ready to guide us through the procedure. There was only one problem—Dad was still conked out. As evening approached, there were several visitors in Dad's room, quietly talking amongst themselves since he was still uncommunicative. I was praying silently, desperate for God to do SOMETHING so that these papers could be signed.

All at once, my father began moving his head around, and his eyes came open. We knew that we needed to be certain Dad was cognizant and fully aware before he would be allowed to sign the legal papers. My father, although still mumbling, then proceeded to greet each of his visitors by name! I asked Dad a few simple questions, which he answered correctly. My father was able to shakily sign his name where needed, and his final wishes could be honored. I thanked God profusely, knowing He had done a miracle.

The next evening, my sister looked at me and said, "Dad isn't saved. You've GOT to do something!" I wanted to know what she suggested I do since Dad had not been awake since he signed those papers twenty-four hours earlier. We prayed, asking God to bring him back to us yet again.

It wasn't long before his eyes popped open wide. I said, "Hi, Dad! Glad to have you back with us." Feeling prompted, I hesitantly asked if he remembered about his cancer and that he didn't have many days left with us. He began nodding as soon as I asked but then began to look terribly afraid. Knowing well this might be the last opportunity, I boldly asked, "Dad, would you like to pray with me to receive Jesus as your Savior?" Clear as a bell and with no hesitation, his answer rang out, "Yes!"

"GLAD TO HAVE YOU BACK WITH US."

I was thrilled as I then had the privilege of leading my dad to Christ. As I would speak a phrase, my father crisply repeated it without mumbling a single word, which amazed both my sister and me. Right after he said, "Amen," he closed his eyes once more, and we never saw him awake again. He passed about a day and a half later.

My siblings and I, along with my husband and our four children, were all gathered in his hospital room singing "Amazing Grace" as he passed into glory. What a joy to know that his last breath here on earth was his first breath in heaven. There is no greater comfort than knowing that a loved one is now home with Jesus!

What about you?

Have you ever had the amazing opportunity to pray with someone to receive salvation?

If so, take some time to thank God for using you in such a mighty way. Then, pray for that person to continue to experience their next steps in Jesus.

If you haven't had that opportunity, pray that God will give you the privilege of leading someone to Him this year.

Wowed by GOD, THE PERFECT REALTOR
by Melanie McGuire

"Now if God so clothes the grass of the field, which today is, and tomorrow is thrown into the oven, will He not much more clothe you, O you of little faith?"
Matthew 6:30 (NKJV)

God had once again called us to another church, and once again, we had a house to sell. As faithful as God had always been to our family, fear still reminded me about the last house that we had to sell and how we struggled for months before it sold. My husband moved to Indiana to begin at our new church while I stayed behind with our girls. I am a teacher, and I needed to finish out the school year, and our oldest daughter was a senior and wanted to graduate with her class. We stayed in our home, prepared it for showings, and prayed for a quick sale.

I wanted it to sell right away so that I wouldn't have to worry about it, but once again, it did not. We put it on the market in March and waited and waited and waited! We were getting down to the end of the school year and still did not have a buyer.

This is what I had feared. It was going to be just like the last time. God called us to a new church but would not sell our house. I prayed and prayed, but doubt still crept in. Finally, we got the call. We had a buyer! We accepted the offer and closed on the very last day of school. We were able to move directly out of our home and to our new home at the same time.

God may not have been early like I wanted Him to be, but He was right on time. We did not have to find a place to live during the last few weeks of school, and we were able to move with all our things at the same time. God's timing is perfect—always!

What about you?

Why do we still doubt when we know God is always faithful?

What journey are you on that looks like another struggle that you have faced before? How can you use your past testimonies to encourage yourself now?

Wowed by OUR PROVIDER
by Christina Shafer

"Do not be anxious about anything, but in everything by prayer and supplication with thanksgiving let your requests be made known to God. And the peace of God, which surpasses all understanding, will guard your hearts and your minds in Christ Jesus." Philippians 4:6-7 (ESV)

There's a time in my marriage that I remember very clearly. My husband Jeremy and I had been married for a little over a year. We didn't have a lot of extra money. We had felt led to leave our jobs and move, and needless to say, money was very tight. We had talked about having kids (and we both knew that we wanted them), but we had agreed to just pray about it during that time. We found jobs, but ones that were barely meeting our needs.

One month in particular, I remember feeling like God was leading us to try for a baby. I expressed this to Jeremy, and to be honest, he struggled. We didn't have a lot. Things were still very tight. I knew that things would have to change if I got **WE DIDN'T HAVE A LOT OF EXTRA MONEY.** pregnant. I would have to quit my job because I was working a physically-taxing job with back-to-back sixteen-plus hour shifts with a high risk of injury. At times, I had to end fights or apply physical restraints on teenage girls. We felt led that if I became pregnant, my time at that job would have to end. I remember Jeremy struggling with my request and saying, "Not yet."

I questioned God and wondered whether I had heard right. *Did you really tell me we should start trying to have a baby soon?* I spent time with the Lord, and it was then that I felt Him lead me to just pray for my husband. I was challenged not to nag him and not to bring up this subject again for at least a couple months. I prayed and released it to the Lord. A couple months later, on his own, Jeremy told me that God was challenging him to trust that He could provide for us. He shared that he had repented and admitted his lack of trust in this area. It was that week that we became pregnant with our son Josiah.

Throughout the pregnancy, things were still hard financially. I remember being about seven to eight months pregnant, and still the nursery sat empty. I felt led one day to write out all the needs that we had, and then to pray and release them to the Lord. As I prayed, I felt such peace. And sure enough, every item on the list was taken care of before my son came.

What about you?

Do you find yourself impatient in an area of your life, struggling with something you'd really like to control?

In Philippians 4:6-7, you are reminded to "not be anxious about anything" and to pray with thanksgiving, so that "the peace of God will guard your hearts and minds." Do you pray with thanksgiving for the needs that are still unmet? Do you run to Him with your needs?

THE PROTECTOR
by Christa Krohn

"From birth I have relied on you; you brought me forth from my mother's womb. I will ever praise you." Psalm 71:6 (NIV)

I have always loved this verse. The idea that the Lord has kept His hand on me from the time I was conceived in my mother's womb makes me feel safe. To know that His hand has been on my children from the time that they were in my womb makes me want to shout praises to His name! The Lord assured me of his protection over my children in a very unique way during the first trimester of my very first pregnancy.

My husband and I were married in June of 1996. We had decided that we were going to take children as they came. I must say that I, probably more than my husband, was ready for them as soon as possible! Six short months had come and gone when I finally got the news I had been waiting for—we were expecting a baby.

At that time, I was working for a credit union and feeling the usual symptoms of an early pregnancy. One evening after coming home from work, I felt some cramping and a sensation of something letting loose in my abdomen. I went to the restroom and saw evidence that I was possibly having a miscarriage. I was heartbroken. I had already shared the good news with my loved ones and was not looking forward to sharing the news of this loss.

The next morning, I called my doctor's office to explain the symptoms I was having, and they said that they believed I had lost the baby, and because it was so early in the pregnancy there was no need to come **I WAS HEARTBROKEN.** in and be seen. My heart was filled with sadness and loss, but I had a feeling the Lord was up to something. For three days, I continued to have symptoms that seemed to confirm a miscarriage, but at the same time I was still feeling pregnant.

On the evening of the third day, I could not sleep. On my knees in my living room I shared my frustration and confusion with the Lord. "Father, what is going on in my body?" I cried. I immediately had the sense of a presence in the room with me, two presences to be exact. The Lord spoke to my heart in that moment. The Lord told me that I was sensing the presence of two guardian angels. One was mine, and the other was the baby's. The Lord said, "The baby is still here, and the baby is fine." I wiped away my tears and returned to bed, falling asleep with a sense of peace that I had not had for days. I was assured of His protection over both of us.

The next morning, I called my doctor's office and explained how I was still feeling. They said I could come in for an examination. Sitting on the doctor's table, I was told that the doctor would try to listen for a heartbeat (even though he had never heard one this early in a pregnancy). The minute he turned on the monitor, the sound of my daughter's strong heartbeat filled the room.

I WAS ASSURED OF HIS PROTECTION OVER BOTH OF US.

I never had another complication with her pregnancy. Today she is a 22-year-old young woman who is loved by God. When she has been overseas, and I am not able to connect with her, the Lord reminds me that the protection He provided for her in the womb is still with her today.

What about you?

Do you believe that the Lord has had His eyes on you since you were in your mother's womb or have the circumstances of your life caused you to feel that He has turned His eyes from you? Do you feel like He has fallen asleep on the job?

Psalms 121:3-4 says, "He will not let your foot slip—he who watches over you will not slumber; indeed, he who watches over Israel will neither slumber nor sleep" (NIV). He has not been asleep on the job. He not only watches over Israel, but He watches over you.

Confess to the Lord today any anger or frustration you may have had with Him over situations in your past when you felt like His protection was absent. Ask Him to open your eyes to see that His presence has been there with you all along.

Wowed by STRAWBERRIES FROM A STRANGER *by Tammy Screws*

"Remember this: Whoever sows sparingly will also reap sparingly, and whoever sows generously will also reap generously. Each of you should give what you have decided in your heart to give, not reluctantly or under compulsion, for God loves a cheerful giver. And God is able to bless you abundantly, so that in all things at all times, having all that you need, you will abound in every good work." 2 Corinthians 9:6-8 (NIV)

It was a crisp, fall Saturday afternoon. This was the first step, the easy part—getting rid of excess stuff from thirteen years of living with my family of five in the same house. We had a yard sale of clothes that the kids had outgrown, things that were in boxes in the basement, and extra items that had been packed away in the shed and not recently used. We were in the process of moving. I had lived in that home with my parents since I was a youth. There were so many memories, and the suddenness and circumstance of the life change that caused us to have to move was not expected, nor pleasant. It was a hard time in our lives.

This beautiful afternoon as we were outside at our yard sale, a lady (who was a complete stranger) stopped by and bought five dollars' worth of stuff. We chatted for a while, and she left—only to return a moment later with a container of fresh strawberries. She said that she had just been to the market and wondered if the kids would like a snack. Their eyes lit up and they all said, "YES, please!" I thanked the lady and washed up the berries to give to my kids who devoured the deliciousness in minutes. Then it hit me, and I teared up.

Through much of my adult life, God had placed us in a profession where we were surrounded by church family. I had lived in the area for much of my life and had many friends. We often were blessed with extra garden produce, meat, supplies, and more. Now as we faced a sudden and unexpected change, I realized that those certain blessings I had come to rely on would no longer be there.

THEN IT HIT ME, AND I TEARED UP.

It was through the gift of strawberries from a stranger that God gently spoke to my heart and reminded me that all of the many blessings through the years had not only come through family and friends, but ultimately came from HIM. He knew exactly where I was, and my situation did not take my God by surprise.

He spoke to me that day that He would be faithful to meet all my needs, and He has continued to come through over and over again.

During that yard sale, I continued to listen to God. There was a couple who really wanted an item, and God told me to sell it to them at half price, so I did. In the end, I made over three times the amount I had expected to make at the sale and enough for a security deposit on my new rental home. It still won't be easy downsizing the rest of our items, but my hope is not in things, but in my Savior. He alone provides for all my needs, and sometimes He uses strangers to do it.

What about you?

How has God met your needs in an unexpected way? Have you thanked Him for it?

God provides generously for you so that you can also provide generously for others. What is one way that you have passed on God's goodness to you to someone else?

It is important to know God personally so that when the storms of life come, you have a shelter in the storm. What have you been doing recently to strengthen your faith?

Wowed by THINGS THAT ARE "ALRIGHT"

by Donna Stocker

"I will answer them before they even call to me. While they are still talking to me about their needs, I will go ahead and answer their prayers." Isaiah 65:24 (NLT)

I had two goals for my life. The first was to be obedient to God's calling, and the second was to be a mother. My husband and I answered the call of God on our lives and entered full-time ministry with the excitement to see where God would lead us and how He could use us. I was equally excited to become a mother which I had dreamed about since I was a little girl. By the age of thirty-six, the Lord had blessed me with three beautiful sons.

By the time my oldest son Ben had gone through his elementary years, they were already filled with challenge after challenge. It became quite apparent that the years ahead could be even more difficult, and difficult they were!

When he was fourteen, we were encouraged to give Ben a timeout from our family structure and allow him to experience time with another family. The hope in him moving was that he would better understand authority, rules, and respect, and realize that they weren't just expectations in our home. He lived in a different state and family setting for just under a year. When he came back into our home, things seemed to only get worse.

I was on my way to church alone one Sunday soon after Ben's re-entry to our home. We had a difficult evening with him the night before. I broke down in utter desperation and cried out to the Lord saying, "If You will tell me it's going to be 'alright,' then I know I can go through anything."

Typically, I sat in the front row with my husband, but not on that morning. Upon entering the sanctuary, I told the Lord I was just going to slip into the back row. I just wanted to be alone. I was feeling so unworthy and like such a parental failure. I even remember saying to the Lord that He should have made me barren.

When the gifts of the Holy Spirit began to minister, a gentleman spoke this Word from the Lord: "There are no back rows in this place, and there is no condemnation in Christ Jesus." I will say that Word got my attention, but I still hadn't heard the words "it's going to be alright." During greeting time, a lady came to me (unaware of our situation) and prefaced her remarks by saying, "I never do this sort of thing." She then continued, "Please don't think this is silly, but the Holy Spirit has compelled me to say only this to you: 'It's going to be alright.'"

From that day until Ben's passing at age forty-two, I have hung onto that Word.

That Word has sustained me with hope so my heart wouldn't be sick. Proverbs 13:12 says, "Hope deferred makes the heart sick, but a dream fulfilled is a tree of life" (NLT). I knew that God keeps His promises.

We walked with Ben through public school, private school, home school, much counseling, addictions, a rehab center called Teen Challenge, jail, prison, a child out of wedlock, and a failed marriage. Thirteen days after our daughter-in-law was diagnosed with colon cancer, we found ourselves burying her. Two years later, Ben passed away. We watched our granddaughter say goodbye to both of her parents at the ages of seven and nine.

On the one-year anniversary weekend of our son's passing, I asked the Lord on a Sunday morning if He would give me fresh assurance that Ben was "alright" with his eternity. Our pastor was teaching on practicing the preference of praise. He talked about how we should praise Him both in the good times as well as in the hard times. God is worthy of our praise just because He's God.

Then, he stopped and said to turn to the one on your left and your right, and tell them, "It's going to be alright." Once again, God heard my cry and gave me the assurance that it was "alright." From the day I walked away from Ben's grave until this day and into my forevermore, the anthem of my heart and soul are these words: *Jesus, Jesus, how I trust you. Oh, for grace to trust you more.* Even in hard, long situations, God is faithful to show us His Glory. I am so grateful to God that He is a personal God who sees us, hears us, and answers our prayers.

IT'S GOING TO BE ALRIGHT.

What about you?

Do you make specific requests to God?

Recall the times you were specific with God, and He was specific with you.

Wowed by HIS DIVINE WARNINGS
by Kelly Rhoads

"Whoever dwells in the shelter of the Most High will rest in the shadow of the Almighty. I will say of the LORD, 'He is my refuge and my fortress, my God in whom I trust.'" Psalms 91:1-2 (NIV)

His plan for us is always good. He is trustworthy and always available—even in the times when we aren't entirely aware of exactly how to pray or what may be around the next corner.

When I was 17, I was attacked by a man that came running up behind me in a parking area that was empty. I was in shock as I turned and saw him, and I couldn't speak. Before he could do what he intended, I finally was able to scream, "NO!" and he ran off. For many years after, if someone ran up behind me, I would freeze and have adrenaline pouring through me. Over time, I learned to let it go, but it was a process. Through that experience, the Holy Spirit began teaching me to be more aware in my life, not just mentally but spiritually as well.

Many years later, I was leaving a mall after closing hours (by myself), and I had to leave through a back hallway. As I opened the door and stepped into this dimly lit hallway, I just "knew" there was danger ahead. I could see the exit door to the parking lot in front of me, but I "knew" I was supposed to turn around and get out. I found an older man who worked there, and he walked me out to my car through another exit. I still don't know what could have happened, but I knew the Holy Spirit was helping me as I trusted Him. He turned that old fear into wisdom as I followed His leading.

Many more years later, my child was away at college. I began to feel this overwhelming, tense emotion. I don't like to confess to fear, but I felt something bad was going on—deep in my bones. It felt like danger was imminent. I felt so helpless as a parent being three hours away. That's when

I JUST "KNEW" THERE WAS DANGER AHEAD.

I began to believe in the power Jesus gave to me, and I began to pray. I began crying out in such a deep way that it turned into deep groanings. I couldn't even think or speak or pray anymore.

After a time, as I literally laid on my kitchen floor, it felt like a huge weight had been lifted. I got up and knew Jesus had intervened and taken care of the situation. I knew the battle had been won, and the danger was over. Although I don't know what specific situation my child was in at the time, I know the Lord once again made me spiritually aware of something I could not see in the natural, and impressed on me the need to intercede and ask for HIS rescuing power.

Isaiah 30:21 says, "Whether you turn to the right or the left, your ears will hear a voice behind you, saying, 'This is the way; walk in it'" (NIV). As we take time to listen to His voice, and to dwell in the shadow of the Almighty, we can rest assured that we will continue to experience His divine direction, warnings, power, and His call to intercede for others.

What about you?

How do we become more spiritually aware of what is going on around us?

Think of a time when you felt an urgent need to intercede for someone or something. Did you obey? What happened?

"Your kingdom is an everlasting kingdom, and your dominion endures through all generations. The LORD is trustworthy in all he promises and faithful in all he does." Psalms 145:13 (NIV)

In 2003, we found out we were pregnant with our second child, and we were, like most parents, overcome with joy. But that joy was quickly diminished because I immediately started having complications with the pregnancy. It didn't help we were living at the time as missionaries in Benin, a country in West Africa with limited medical facilities. My French doctor did her very best job caring for me, but the next few months were the most difficult ones I had ever experienced.

Despite the fact that I was taking close to twenty pills a day, my complications continued. There were many times when I thought I had lost our baby. I had been on bed rest for months and had already been admitted to the hospital once (where I watched ants and lizards climb the walls in my room). On top of all that, I had already contracted malaria twice, a disease that can easily affect an unborn baby. I felt like I was on a tiny boat in the middle of a raging ocean. I was physically and emotionally exhausted.

It was in the midst of all the chaos that God gave me a promise. He said, "Lacei, you are going to have a beautiful, healthy baby." Although I desperately wanted to believe those words, I have to admit that I struggled with them. Everything else—medical knowledge and human logic—said the exact opposite. My

I WAS ON A TINY BOAT IN THE MIDDLE OF A RAGING OCEAN.

French doctor told me that if my pregnancy continued, she was almost certain the baby wouldn't make it to full term. The medical professionals couldn't even figure out how to keep me from having contractions, and I was still in my first trimester.

Yet, I knew God had given me this promise, so I tried to look past what I could see in the natural, and believe God for the supernatural. Some days I walked in faith, believing and trusting God for what seemed to be the impossible. Other days I walked in fear and worry, tears streaming down my face as I felt yet another contraction or had to swallow yet another pill. The doctors continued to tell me all the things that were wrong with me, all the reasons why the hope of carrying this baby to full term was not very realistic.

When I was five months along, we were able to travel back to the United

States on medical furlough. I continued to be on bed rest until I was thirty-seven weeks along—a total of seven months, and then our baby boy was born through scheduled C-section at thirty-nine weeks—completely healthy and malaria free. He was a true miracle of God and a promise fulfilled.

Even though it seemed like my tiny boat might capsize at any time, He never let the waves engulf me. Even though I felt pretty wet sometimes, He never failed to wrap that warm towel around me and just hold me in His arms, all the while reassuring me that He would never leave me or forsake me. Although that season was an extremely difficult one, I learned that I can always trust Him—no matter the circumstances. He will do what He says He will do.

What about you?

What are some promises that God has given you?

On a scale of 1-5 (with 5 being complete and total trust), how much faith do you honestly have that He will keep those promises?

How can you increase your trust in Him when circumstances cause you to doubt?

Wowed by HIS MERCY TOWARDS ME
by Karen Prevost

"But he gives more grace. Therefore it says, 'God opposes the proud, but gives grace to the humble.'" James 4:6 (ESV)

I am a snob. I didn't realize it at first. Jesus revealed it to me as He answered a question I had. Let me explain how it happened.

I was working with someone I had just met and didn't know very well. She was actually very kind and generous, and she was willing to serve in any capacity. She never did anything to offend me and was a hard worker. Sounds like a good situation, so what was the problem? Actually, I was.

I allowed some "thought seeds" to enter my mind, seemingly inoffensive thoughts like, *She's kind of "different." She looks "different." Her personality is "different."* As I kept repeating phrases like this to myself, the "thought seeds" slipped down into my heart and started to grow. I found myself feeling irritated by her for no apparent reason. I didn't enjoy being with her and looked for excuses to be somewhere else when she was around.

I knew something was wrong, and from experience I knew that when I am bothered inside, the problem is inside of me. But I wasn't sure exactly what the problem was. So I asked Jesus, "Why am I feeling this way?" The answer came immediately: "Because you think you are better than she is." Ouch. I knew Jesus was right.

Just days later, I read this in Luke 18:9: "To some who were confident of their own righteousness AND LOOKED DOWN ON EVERYBODY ELSE, Jesus told this parable" (NIV). The Pharisee in the parable told God how much better he was than others, especially the tax collector. The tax collector just called on God to have mercy on him for all of his sins. I knew I was the Pharisee in this story.

SO I ASKED JESUS, "WHY AM I FEELING THIS WAY?"

When I look down on others, I am trusting in myself. I put my confidence in my own works. When I think I am better than others, that is pure pride. I began calling out to God, "Forgive me for thinking I am better than anyone else. I am not. I am a recipient of the same grace and mercy You offer to everyone else." God forgave me and softened my heart.

I started off like the Pharisee, thinking I was better than someone else. But I ended up like the tax collector, crying out for God's mercy because of my sinful pride. I am still in the parable, but this time, praise God, I am the tax collector. I am in desperate need of His mercy and grace. I do not want to be a snob anymore.

What about you?

When have you thought you were better than others? Repent of your pride, and ask for God's mercy to change your heart, too.

Pray a blessing over the ones you have looked down on, and thank God for them.

Wowed by HIS BEAUTIFUL BODY
by Glenda Olson

"**Each of you should use whatever gift you have received to serve others, as faithful stewards of God's grace in its various forms.**" 1 Peter 4:10 (NIV)

It was an early morning in Nashville, and we were sitting in my car outside of Kroger. I was with my stepmom (who also happens to be one of my closest friends), and we were deep in conversation. I had started to cry as I poured out my heart to Heidi. I was feeling profoundly weary at that time in my life. It's hard to put into words all the things that led me to that place except to say it felt like I was "waiting on God" in so many areas of my life. I have a high capacity and a deep faith, so though He was sustaining me through it all, it was a hard daily walk.

I think the thing that was the most difficult to bear was that I had a deep desire for us to start our family, but both Mike and I had sensed that God said, "Not yet." That "waiting" was the one thing that would make me cry in the shower as I cried out to Him. I trusted Him and His perfect timing, and yet it hurt deeper than I knew possible as I longed for this little person I didn't even know.

IT WAS A HARD DAILY WALK.

As I was sharing all of this with Heidi, I gripped the steering wheel with both of my hands and through the tears I said, "I can keep going as long as I know that He is in control!" Heidi assured me that He was and started to pray for me to know that He was all-powerful. She declared that He saw me, loved me, and He had good plans for me and Mike—and our future family.

As she was praying, we heard a knock. Both of us jumped a bit as we opened our eyes to see a woman standing at my door. I rolled down my window, and with a bit of a quivering voice, she said, "I was walking past your car, and I felt the Lord tell me to stop and tell you that He has the wheel. He is in control. I hope that blesses you!" And she was gone.

Heidi and I sat there in a stunned silence for several seconds, and then we both burst out praising and laughing with joy. Heidi raised her arms as she praised Him right there in the passenger seat for what He had just done. How could we do anything but praise the One who sees and knows and who activates His body (His people) to be His hands and feet?

We quickly ran into the grocery store to grab the few things we needed, and I looked around to find that woman and to thank her. I was half expecting not to find her because she was an angel, but that was not the case this time. I found her in the frozen food aisle. I went up to her to thank her, and as I told her the whole story, a huge grin spread across her face, and she stood up a little bit taller.

She told me how she had never done anything like this before, but the past week at church her pastor had challenged the church to be willing to minister to people when they were out and about the next week. She said she was a bit scared, but when she walked by my car, she knew she had to do it. She was so built up to hear that because of her faithfulness, He used her to specifically and powerfully minister to a sister in Christ. Three women left the store that day with a deeper trust in God, in His control, and in how He wants to use His body to build up others.

What about you?

Recall a time when someone in the body of Christ was used by God to minister deeply to you. If you have a way to contact that person, reach out to him or her and say thanks for being faithful to use his or her gifts to bless you.

Pray and ask God if there is anyone that He wants you to reach out to with a word of encouragement, a scripture, or a prayer. Be faithful and do what He asks of you, trusting that He knows just what that person needs.

Wowed by SUFFERING
by Kyja Malone

"Rejoice always, pray continually, give thanks in all circumstances, for this is God's will for you in Christ Jesus." 1 Thessalonians 5:16-18 (NIV)

Suffering and thankfulness don't usually go together. Surely this verse doesn't mean ALL circumstances, right? What about when my thirty-four-year-old husband is diagnosed with an aggressive form of cancer? Do I need to give thanks in that circumstance? What about when I have a newborn along with my two other children, and now my husband is in the hospital for multiple days at a time getting chemo, and I feel like a single parent most of the time? Do I give thanks for that? What about when my five-year-old daughter asks me if her daddy is going to die? Do I give thanks in that circumstance? Who would ever be thankful for suffering? As it turns out—me! I am wowed by suffering, and God has helped me to be thankful in the midst of it all.

I AM THANKFUL FOR SUFFERING because it reminds me of my daily need for Jesus and how I must rely on Him completely for everything. I can't do it on my own. I'm weak, and especially in times of difficulty, I can get distracted or sad or lazy and not go to the source of all comfort, of all peace, of all strength. In times of suffering, we are brought to our knees out of desperation for God to move—to heal, to forgive, to rescue. In my suffering, I am forced to my knees, and that is where I want to stay.

I AM THANKFUL FOR SUFFERING because it has built my faith. My heart overflowed from the kindness of people, the generosity, the support, the prayers, and the scriptures that were sent from God's people. God showed Himself faithful to me through so many believers. There were multiple times when I received the same scripture from different people who lived in different states at the same time (because God loves me that much and knew I needed a reminder). He also showed himself faithful through His perfect timing. My husband, Michael, was released from the hospital the very night before our daughter started kindergarten. Finally, He showed Himself faithful through provision. Every need we had, financial or otherwise, was met. Time and time again, God built my faith as we experienced Him do what only He could do.

I AM THANKFUL FOR SUFFERING because God has given me boldness to share about His goodness more than ever before. Michael and I began sharing parts of our journey on Facebook with live events in which we always went back to Scripture and the gospel. I had conversations with friends and family and even people I didn't know about the importance of Jesus in our lives. We were given so many different opportunities to share our story of God's goodness in all things. Even writing this might not have happened a year ago, but God has opened doors for us to be bold and share our part in His story!

I AM THANKFUL FOR SUFFERING because it refocuses me on the things that truly matter. It forces me to have an eternity mindset, to consider death more than I ever had before. When you think about life and death and heaven and hell, you start to shift your priorities. More than ever, I feel the importance of bringing my kids up with the Word of God and pointing them to a relationship with Jesus Christ. I feel the urgency of sharing the gospel with those who have not yet heard. I feel freed from the trap of needing more and bigger and better "stuff" because I already, in Christ, have everything I will ever need. All my "stuff" can't come with me, but I strive and pray that my children and family and friends and everyone I know will walk into heaven with me. What a blessing to have an eternity mindset.

Now don't get me wrong; suffering is real, and it is hard. God's original design did not include suffering, but since He is good, He takes the bad and turns it into something great. He makes beauty from ashes. He redeems, He restores, He renews. He promises in 2 Corinthians 4:17 that "this light momentary affliction is preparing for us an eternal weight of glory beyond all comparison" (ESV). When you walk through troubles with faith in Christ, they are always producing for you good things both now and in eternity. Yes, there is suffering, but God gets the mic drop.

What about you?

What suffering have you endured?

What is something you are thankful for that came out of it?

Wowed by THE ONE WHO SETS ME FREE
by Kristine Rusch

"We demolish arguments and every pretension that sets itself up against the knowledge of God, and we take captive every thought to make it obedient to Christ." 2 Corinthians 10:5 (NIV)

Growing up in the church, I had read 2 Corinthians 10:5 often and thought I kind of knew what it meant. But, it was not until I truly experienced it that I truly understood. Let me explain.

It was March of 2016, and Nicole, our youngest daughter, was pregnant with our first grandchild! She and her husband Michael were so excited to have a baby, and when she went into labor, things seemed to be moving rather well. I was so proud of her and how she was handling it. Then, the nurse flopped her from one side to the next and suddenly pushed the call button which sent many nurses running into Nicole's room—rushing my husband and I out in the process.

This mama's heart was trying hard not to panic, but the tears rolled down my cheeks, completely out of my control. I immediately texted some intercessors asking for prayer. I can't tell you word for word what each replied, but one replied with the lyrics to the song, "It is Well With My Soul." Knowing the author of that song wrote it after losing his four daughters, I wasn't sure I wanted to hear that, but my husband Pat looked into my eyes and reminded me that regardless of the background of that song, we needed to pray for Nicole and be "well with our souls."

As we prayed and waited, I began thinking about that song, and I realized that every time we sing that song, as soon as we begin to sing that first word, I begin to intercede for each one of my kids, and fear begins to creep in. I wasn't sure why this seemed to always be the case. So, the Lord and I began to have a conversation about this song and why it seemed to freak me out. *Did I trust Him? Did I trust that if anything happened to my kids and they would pass away without me being at their side that He'd be with me, and it would be "well with my soul"?* I wasn't sure that I could say yes. So, I had to dig a little deeper to find out why.

And here's what I think it was: I needed to know that each one of my girls had a personal relationship with the Lord Jesus and that they had actually physically asked Him to be Lord of their life. As a PK (pastor's kid) I didn't want them to think that they'd get into heaven just because of my relationship with the Lord, or their dad's position of being a pastor, or just because they're sitting in the church warming their spot in the pew and going through the motions. I wanted to know they were truly right with the Lord.

So, at different times (after my beautiful, healthy granddaughter was born) I had conversations with each one of my daughters, and they each assured me that they had physically asked Jesus to be Lord of their lives. I didn't need to live in fear of what might happen to them if they passed into eternity. They would be with Jesus. So, when I have those thoughts, I have to take them captive, rest in truth, and choose to continue to walk in freedom from fear when the enemy sends thoughts my way.

Just recently, I was praying for protection over Nicole, Michael, and my now two granddaughters while they were on vacation, asking the Lord to keep each one of them safe while they were traveling and then to protect the girls as they played around the lake. All of a sudden, I found myself praying with a fearful heart. I began having visions of things going wrong on their trip—and then I caught myself! I realized what was happening and that I had to "take captive every thought and make it obedient to Christ."

I actually began DOING this scripture verse. I began to quote 2 Corinthians 10:5 and also 2 Timothy 1:7: "For God has not given us the spirit of fear, but of power and of love and of a sound mind" (NKJV). Then, I went back to praying over them, knowing that I had just wielded the sword (the Word of God) and put the devil in his place (under my feet).

The title to this devotion is "Wowed by the One Who Sets Me Free." Honestly, I can't say that I'm walking in this freedom every moment of every day. But I can tell you that when I begin to fear something negative, I HAVE TO take captive those thoughts and I HAVE TO make them obedient to Christ. That's where I find freedom—His freedom.

What about you?

Are you currently struggling with fearful thoughts?

Take time to write them down in your journal, but don't stop there. Write out 2 Corinthians 10:5 and 2 Timothy 1:7, and then pray those scriptures over your fears!

Wowed by GOD'S PLANS
by Jennifer Miller

"Direct me in the path of your commands, for there I find delight." Psalms 119:35 (NIV)

You are on a trail enjoying the beauty of all that surrounds you, and your guide says, "Turn down here." You think the guide must be crazy because it's a narrow and rough path—not pretty and easy like the one you are on currently. You want to trust, and you want adventure, but this path you are walking on now is nice. All the questions come: *Can I do it? Am I prepared? Will I be carrying others back when they can't make it? Do I even want to work THAT hard?* Sometimes just the questions can stop us from even trying the new path. It's not even our fears necessarily that hinder our obedience, but rather us getting overwhelmed by life, our plans, and the normal paths all around us.

Walk with me a bit as I tell you about where I've walked. Maybe our trails and paths will seem familiar, or maybe it will give you insight as you move forward on your own path. When my husband and I got married, we had a nifty five-year plan (as any good twenty-somethings who had just graduated college have). We quickly found that as we trusted God for our path together, we had to be prepared for turns and twists we couldn't see at the start of the journey. At first, they were easy path changes. They were different, but the view was still good. Then, we decided that we'd start a family. Why not? It seemed reasonable. That is what other married people did at this point in their journey.

After a year of this journey to start a family, our path had clearly changed. What once was a smooth, easy trail turned into a narrower, rocky path. It wasn't clear, and it was harder to walk. Everything seemed heavier, and we had to depend on each other in a different way than ever before. We started talking to doctors and doing tests. That journey went on for over five years. We went down side paths, thinking they would get us where we wanted to be, but they just led to dead ends.

Finally, in July of 2009, at one of our last appointments, a doctor gave us our last option, which we had already decided was beyond what we knew we should do. We knew the path God had asked us to walk, and this doctor was showing us a path we knew we couldn't go down. I remember so clearly having to turn around, having to close that door. I wept as I realized that I had no idea how we would get to our perceived destination. We had also explored a few adoption options, but they just weren't right for us—yet another turn on this already rocky path.

We had prayed often during these five years and asked God to guide our steps. We asked for wisdom and bravery. We had begged God for a child, but we ultimately longed for His will. We submitted our hearts and behavior to His plan and not our plan. We knew in the depth of our hearts, past all the norms of society and all the advice of humans, that honoring God and walking His path would bring us to the best destinations.

We had no clue where we were going at this point, but we knew that His Word is a lamp to guide our feet and a light for our path (Psalms 119:105). As we had done many times before, we adjusted our stance and moved forward. We focused on what we knew was God's plan—meet the needs in front of you and love the world you are placed in. We clearly could not make our plans work, but we could lean into His plans.

In October 2009, the path started changing. A friend asked if we might be interested in adoption and connected us to a family member. It was like a dream. It was like the sun started to shine on the path again. As my husband and I talked, we realized that God had been working all along. He had been smoothing out that path before us.

He had taken us the long way so that we would be safe and prepared, like the Israelites. He was planning our paths to merge with our daughter's at just the right time: "Your eyes saw my unformed body; all the days ordained for me were written in your book before one of them came to be" (Psalms 139:16, NIV). Had we listened to other voices or turned down the seemingly easier paths, we would not have known the joy and blessing of our daughter. Seven years after our oldest daughter was born, we gave birth to our second child. We now have two beautiful daughters with unbelievable stories to tell of God's faithful journey and His story.

What about you?

What does your path look and feel like right now? Be honest.

Have you walked down "good" paths but not the best paths?

Take time and ask God for courage to hear and respond to His voice, praying Psalms 25:4, "Show me your ways, LORD, teach me your paths." (NIV)

THE ONE WHO NEVER ABANDONS *by Christa Krohn*

Wowed by

"Moses answered the people, 'Do not be afraid. Stand firm and you will see the deliverance the LORD will bring you today.'" Exodus 14:13 (NIV)

In Exodus chapter 14, the Israelites were caught between the Red Sea and Pharaoh's army, after being freed from captivity in Egypt. They had just been set free from captivity in Egypt. Pharaoh, having second thoughts about releasing his workforce, was hot on their trail. The Israelites were complaining to Moses that it would have been better for them to serve the Egyptians than to die in the desert. But the Lord had not led them to that place to die; He was not going to abandon them on this side of the Red Sea. He had other plans—as He often does. Four years ago, during a difficult season in my life, I got a glimpse of some of His "other plans." The Lord went out of His way to remind me that He did not bring me this far in life to abandon me where I was.

Since as far back as I can remember I have always had trouble eating. Almost every time I ate, I would feel sick to my stomach. It was never, IF I would feel sick, but WHEN. From the time I was a child, I dreaded social situations when a meal was involved. I learned tricks to make it seem like I was eating so that I would not stand out. Since I had to choose between feeling sick or feeling hungry, I chose feeling hungry. This led to many problems; one was an over-exaggerated focus on food and a fear of how eating made me feel. The other was that I was always extremely underweight and unhealthy.

Over the years I saw doctors and had multiple tests to see what was causing this issue to no avail. One of these doctors told my mother that it was all in my head. So that is what I chose to believe, that I had an atypical eating disorder. This thought process brought with it a lot of shame and a feeling of hopelessness that I was never going to have victory over this situation in my life.

The summer before I turned forty-one, I started having pain and indigestion even when drinking liquids. My doctor started treating me for an ulcer which brought some relief, but I was so discouraged. As the Christmas season approached, I found myself at home one evening crying out to the Lord. My children and husband were at a dress rehearsal for our church's Christmas production. It was a rare moment of quiet in front of our Christmas tree as I poured out my heart to the Lord. All my fears that something was severely wrong and that I was going to keep losing weight and eventually die came pouring out. I had prayed for healing for so long. I had tried counseling and different medications along with multiple eating plans, and nothing seemed to be helping. *Why wasn't He answering my cries?*

At that moment I heard Him say, "Don't give up. Your healing is coming." I felt some encouragement from those words but wondered if it was just wishful thinking on my part. Later, I went to watch the end of the dress rehearsal. The music director had commissioned some paintings by an artist in our congregation that depicted different scenes from the Bible. They were displayed and would later be available for sale. When a painting of the Israelites crossing the Red Sea came on the screens, the Lord spoke to my heart again: "Don't give up. I did not bring you this far in life to abandon you on the far side of the sea. Your healing is coming."

A few days later I was having another challenging morning and feeling hopeless again. During my devotional time the Lord again said, "Don't give up." In my mind I saw that painting, and I heard Him say, "I am going to give you that painting for Christmas, and every time you see it, you will be reminded of My promise to not abandon you." I had not asked anyone for it as a gift. I had previously inquired as to how much that painting would cost. It was way out of my budget and out of the budget of anyone who would be buying me a gift. But I have learned that God does not have a budget when it comes to going above and beyond to remind His children of His care for them.

You can guess how the story ends. One week later a friend of mine gave me an early Christmas gift. It was the painting! It hangs in my dining room as a reminder of His promise that He did not bring me this far to abandon me. And you know what? He kept that promise. Less than eight months later, I was healed in a way I never saw coming. But that is a story for another day.

What about you?

Are you in a season of life when it feels like the Lord has abandoned you? Do you feel that He lacks the strength or the will to see you through to the other side?

Exodus 14:14 says, "The Lord will fight for you; you need only to be still" (NIV). If He could part the Red Sea to take the Israelites through to the other side, He will see you through as well. Take some quiet moments to reflect on the Lord's promises to you and thank Him for always being faithful to keep them.

Wowed by THE MORE-THAN-ENOUGH GOD

by Pam Wellington

"Jesus Christ is the same yesterday and today and forever." Hebrews 13:8 (NIV)

Years ago, as a new believer, I was learning to pray and trust God for answers. Our children were young, and paychecks never stretched quite far enough each month—especially if one of the kids needed new shoes or required a trip to the doctor. One particular day, knowing that our food supply was getting low, I opened the freezer compartment to select something to thaw and prepare for dinner later.

I was shocked by the reality that the ground beef I was removing would be the very last package of any meat we had on hand, and payday was still several days away. The freezer also held one or two loaves of bread from the last trip to the bargain bread store. And that was it. An inventory of the kitchen cupboards' meager offerings began scrolling through my mind, and I felt the familiar panic begin to rise. Then a new idea came: Why don't you pray about this?

Honestly, my first thought was *Really? Pray about groceries?* But then the second thought was *Well, why not?* I wasn't yet familiar with much of what the Bible had to say, but I did know the story of the loaves and fishes. I had also recently read that Jesus is the same yesterday, and today and forever. So, I prayed, "Father God, You know our need here. Rather than worrying about this

PRAY ABOUT GROCERIES?

like I normally would and getting all stressed out, I'm asking You to provide for us. You know we are going to run out of food before the next paycheck. Please have someone bring us a few groceries or—well, I guess I'll leave the HOW up to you as well. In Jesus' name. Amen."

I had no sooner shut the freezer door and walked across our kitchen floor when the telephone began ringing in the adjoining dining room. (Think old-school phone sitting on an actual phone table!) I answered the phone, "Hello?" "I'd like to speak to Pam, please," the female voice requested. I stated, "This is Pam," wondering who this was. *Another pesky salesperson?*

"Well, Pam, my name is Doris. I'm the manager at your local Harding's Grocery Store, and it must be your lucky day! Your name has just been drawn as the winner of the gift certificate we are giving away!"

Having no immediate memory of actually filling out the entry card several days before, I was confused for just a split second. (Grocery shopping with three little ones in tow isn't the calmest time, for certain.) But I quickly recovered, responding, "That's wonderful news! Praise Jesus! Thank you so very much, Doris!"

Doris then gave me instructions on picking up the certificate at the customer service desk the next time I came in. She further explained that I could then select whatever items I wanted and simply hand the paper to the cashier at the checkout. Little did Doris know how very soon that would take place! I hung up, marveling at how quickly the Lord had answered and in a way that I never could have anticipated. Isn't that often the case concerning His answers to our urgent prayers?

The amount of that prize would seem meager by today's standards. But as I said at the beginning, this was YEARS ago. I looked it up and the current equivalent would be sixty dollars! That certificate provided many groceries that I picked up later that same day. In fact, they lasted BEYOND our next payday. I was beginning to grasp in my new walk of faith that God not only hears and answers prayer, but that He is a more-than-enough God as well.

What about you?

Have you ever experienced a miracle?

What was the first miracle you remember experiencing?

What are some things that you know you need to give to God, trusting that He is more than enough to handle them?

HIS LIGHT IN A YEAR OF BROKENNESS

Wowed by *by Wendy Elarton*

"Send me your light and your faithful care; let them bring me to your holy mountain, to the place where you dwell. Then I will go to the altar of God, to God my joy, and my delight. I will praise you with the lyre, O God, my God. Why, my soul are you downcast? Why so disturbed within me? Put your hope in God, for I will yet praise him, my Savior and my God." Psalms 43:3-5 (NIV)

When I look back ten years ago, I am reminded of a year of brokenness for me and my family. Opening an old journal from the middle of that year, I saw my own words about that season: "Eleven really hard things have changed our lives from easy to hard." As I read over the list, I noticed that three of the complications had been fixed over time, and the inconveniences and expenses were not that bad. The eight others were the ones that brought me to a brokenness like I had never experienced before.

It started right at the beginning of the year; we said goodbye to my husband's spiritual hero, his older brother Steve. This man had a mighty impact on my man. There were always words of wisdom and encouragement flowing from his mouth to bring my preacher-man husband up to a higher level. Steve had an enormous impact on our children also. Loss through death was a frequent part of being in a church family, but when this spiritual giant died, the tragic loss shook a nerve in all of our hearts. We could not even offer support and words of hope for his family. It was so difficult.

Yes, we knew God had made the decision to take this godly man home, but we had so desperately cried out for healing. *Why would God allow a middle-aged man who had recently become a grandparent to be separated from his wife?* We had watched their deep love for each other and care; a lot of their example of marriage helped form ours. Though our hearts ached, we knew they didn't ache

WE COULD NOT EVEN OFFER SUPPORT AND WORDS OF HOPE FOR HIS FAMILY.

nearly as badly as what his family was experiencing. When our hearts can't move past the broken feelings, God allows us to ask "why" and feel darkness. *Was He not there?* Answers did not come. Yet, I knew with my head knowledge the truth about God's character and what His Word promises: He will never leave me nor forsake me (Deuteronomy 31:8).

I continued to move through that year with a crippled heart. The journal entry on the fourth of May started with Matthew 21:43-44: "Therefore I tell you that the kingdom of God will be taken away from you and given to a people who produce its fruit. Anyone who falls on this stone will be broken to pieces; anyone on whom it falls will be crushed" (NIV).

So, my prayer went like this: "Father, I want to humbly fall on You and be broken to pieces. May my heart be humbled before You. I see now You may want me to stay in this broken state." Wow. This was the Holy Spirit leading me in this prayer. I wrote the list of eleven things, but I also realized how much God cared because the next page was filled with twenty things to praise Him for.

That year was a time of adjusting to loss and uncomfortable goodbyes. The seven other things were not the deaths of others, but an abyss of unreasonable changes with people we loved. Again and again, we needed to remember the only One who is always there is God. As I remember back to the days and days of darkness, and I recall the sadness, confusion, regret, unfairness, and complications beyond our control, I know God never left us.

Psalms 91:14 gives us a glimpse of what God says to us in our brokenness: "I will rescue those who love me. I will protect those who trust in my name" (NLT). The heart can become so heavy and broken, but when we remember and continue to trust in His name, our God will protect, deliver, and lighten the path. I am wowed by God's ways of healing our hurts and revealing how He has held us through it all—His light in the midst of the brokenness. Praise Him!

What about you?

Are you going through a year of brokenness, or have you gone through one in the past?

Take time right now to write down some things that He has done for you this year. Thank Him for His light in the midst of brokenness.

WEIGHT GAIN
by Tammy Screws

"Then Peter said, 'Silver or gold I do not have, but what I do have I give you. In the name of Jesus Christ of Nazareth, walk.' Taking him by the right hand, he helped him up, and instantly the man's feet and ankles became strong. He jumped to his feet and began to walk. Then he went with them into the temple courts, walking and jumping and praising God. When all the people saw him walking and praising God, they recognized him as the same man who used to sit begging at the temple gate called Beautiful, and they were filled with wonder and amazement at what had happened to him. . . many who heard the message believed; so the number of men who believed grew to about five thousand." Acts 3:6-10, 4:4 (NIV)

Have you ever been the one to hold your child's hair back as she throws up? As a mother, there is something extra difficult about seeing one of your children suffering and not being able to fix it. We spent much of my daughter's kindergarten year at doctors' offices. I remember (all too often) trying to comfort this little body as she was on the floor in the bathroom—sometimes just heaving, even though there was nothing left to come out.

I recall her crying and holding her stomach because she was so hungry, but still feeling so sick that she had to excuse herself twice during a meal to go to the bathroom. She was so thin that she could easily zip her two-year-old brother's jacket onto her frail frame. She went through test after test and saw specialist after specialist

> **WE SPENT MUCH OF MY DAUGHTER'S KINDERGARTEN YEAR AT DOCTOR'S OFFICES.**

until finally, she was diagnosed with severe acid reflux. I saw the screen as the technician maneuvered her for this test. I also personally saw what he confirmed. Nothing would stay down.

The physician who interpreted these test results sent our daughter to a children's hospital for a pH probe. We were told that a tube would be placed up her nose, down her throat, and into her stomach, all while this five-year-old was conscious—and it had to remain there for 24 hours to record. I was a mess. I went to worship practice at church, and the ladies on the team gathered around and prayed (again). This time it felt different; we had prayed many times before, but this time, I had a renewed peace.

Though we still had to drive awhile for the test, God miraculously provided money to cover the cost of our lodging, meals, and gas! Our daughter was able to get the tube in, and we made it through the next twenty-four hours (with little sleep). When we returned to the specialist for the results, I was shocked. He said that there was no indication of acid reflux or of any issues! He said that he simply could not explain why, but he gave me a script for medicine to give her "for her pain."

I made a follow up appointment with my child's pediatrician who had been walking with us through this difficult time. After reviewing all of the tests and results, she declared that the specialist simply "did not know how to handle the healing of our God!" She also took the script and tore it up and said that the medication prescribed was an addictive narcotic and would not be necessary. I am thankful for Christian doctors. She was right. The Lord healed our child. *But why then? Why not the first time we prayed? Why did she have to suffer so much first?*

In Acts chapter 3, Peter and John were going to the temple at the time of prayer. There was a man who was crippled from birth who was carried to the gate to beg. Peter and John called to him and commanded his healing "in the name of Jesus." Consider this: Was this the first time that Peter and John had gone to the temple? Probably not. Was this the first time that this man was there begging? I don't believe so. Had Jesus himself perhaps passed by this man at the gate? It is quite possible! So why did this miracle happen when it did and not sooner?

All I know is that God's ways and timing are not ours, but they are infinitely greater. He can take our times of suffering and weave them together for His purposes. What if there were certain onlookers that day who needed evidence that Jesus had risen and was the Messiah, and this miracle sealed their faith? It certainly became a testimony for the disciples. What if my daughter's story was a testimony to one of the many doctors and nurses she saw?

I once sat in a Sunday School class taught by an EMT who also had a Biblical Studies degree. He said that a believer's healing is guaranteed. He taught that there are four ways that God chooses to heal: an instant miracle, a progressive miracle, through the power of medicine and wisdom of doctors, or in eternity with our glorified body. If you are a believer in Jesus, take heart that you too will be healed!

Six years later my daughter is a happy and

HE CAN TAKE OUR TIMES OF SUFFERING AND WEAVE THEM TOGETHER FOR HIS PURPOSES.

HEALTHY middle schooler who is nearly as tall as me and who can eat nearly as much as her father (especially during a growth spurt)! We are wowed by her weight gain and most of all by the healing work of our God!

What about you?

Have you been asking God for healing for yourself or someone else?

How has He answered your prayer? (If you have a personal relationship with Jesus, remind yourself that your healing is guaranteed—maybe just not in your own timing.)

How can knowing God is in control give you peace to endure through hard times?

owed by THE RICHES OF HIS GLORY
by Lisa Homrich

"And my God will meet all your needs according to the riches of His glory in Christ Jesus." Philippians 4:19 (NIV)

When my family and I went to bed on Monday, May 18, 2020, we knew our city of Midland was going to get a lot of rain, and that many houses in our area were going to flood. We weren't too worried about our house though, because the last time it had flooded (in 2017), our house only got about six inches of water in the basement. So, our family slept pretty well that night.

In the morning, my four-year-old son, Brayden, woke up at his usual time—way earlier than I ever want to get up. As we made our way downstairs, I could see a reflection of light coming from the road outside our house. The moment I could see out the window, it was clear that our neighborhood had in fact flooded the night before. Immediately, I ran upstairs to wake my husband, David, up. "There's water in the road in front of the house! It's almost into our yard!" It didn't take David long to run down the stairs so he could properly assess the situation at hand.

The three of us watched as our neighbor packed up his car, along with his wife and daughter, and attempted to drive through the flood waters. David and I decided that if our neighbor could make it out, we needed to pack up our kids and whatever we could take with us and get out of the house before it was too late. As we watched our neighbors make it out safely, my phone went off. It was now 7:50am, and I was getting a text from another one of our neighbors. She told me that water was pouring into their basement.

We knew we had to act fast, so before we packed up our kids, we went down to the basement and started taking things up off the floor. We thought that if we could just get our things at least a foot off the floor, everything would be safe. Then, it was time to get our kids, clothes and any other essentials into the car. Once we made it out safely, we were somewhat relieved.

But then came another awful reality: we had no place to go. This is where God began to step in and do what only He can do. Some friends not only volunteered to help us try to save the things in our house, but they also let us stay in their home for the next eight days! While we were at their house on Tuesday night, an alert went off to inform us that a dam had failed. It was in this moment that we knew that there was now no hope of our house staying dry. The flooding was inevitable. We had heard this alert a few times during this crazy event and to be honest, it has quickly become one of my least favorite sounds in the world. I've heard it once or twice after the flood, and the sound of it still makes my stomach drop.

The next day, David and I had to go to work. Though our house was weighing heavy on our minds, there wasn't much we could do because the flood had made it near impossible to even get to the house. I say "near impossible" because two of our friends were in fact able to canoe over to it. Once they got there, they called us on FaceTime.

What we saw next was one of the most heart wrenching things I've ever experienced. The water had risen so high, it was almost halfway up our garage door. I watched from my phone as they rowed the canoe up to the playroom window. When they put their phone up to it so we could see inside, the tears began to flow. I could see our possessions floating around! Not only had our basement flooded, but we also had water on our main floor. David and I were completely devastated.

The first few nights after seeing our house under water were terrible. Every time I closed my eyes, all I could see was the water in my house. I cried myself to sleep. I felt helpless, hopeless, and lost. God was providing, but I knew that the road ahead would be long and exhausting. Over the next few days, and even weeks, we watched as countless numbers of people stepped in to help us. They did everything from helping carry things out, to knocking out walls so we could properly dry our house. Then came the cards, and the toys for our boys, and the meals, and the donations of money.

David and I started to feel guilty. So many people had been hit by this flood (about 10,000 homes), and we are pastors. We are supposed to serve others and to meet other's needs. We had never really been on the receiving end like this before. And yet, here we were. As I sat there thinking, God spoke to me: "It's your turn. You have blessed others so much; now, let others bless you." The more I think about all of the ways we have been blessed, the more I am wowed by the One.

God has always supplied our needs. He's always gone above and beyond. But until this moment in time, I had never fully experienced what it meant for Him to supply according to HIS riches and glory. Every good and perfect thing belongs to God. The stock of riches He has at His disposal is endless. The greater the devastation, the greater the opportunity for God to show up and show off. Two people shared with us at two separate times that they felt God was going to restore everything back to us, better than it was before, and that we wouldn't pay anything out of our own pocket for any of it. This is the reality we are living in right now. God is meeting our needs according to the riches of His glory.

What about you?

How rich is God? How does it make you feel to know that He meets ALL of our needs according to the riches of His glory?

How does this Scripture speak to our worry and anxiety?

Wowed by HIS IMMEASURABLY MORE
by Lacei Grabill

"Now to Him who is able to do immeasurably more than all we ask or imagine, according to His power that is at work within us, to Him be the glory in the church and in Christ Jesus throughout all generations, forever and ever! Amen." Ephesians 3:20-21 (NIV)

I absolutely love this verse. It's been a favorite of mine for years. I am both intrigued and perplexed by it. God is able to do immeasurably more than we can ask for, even more than our minds can conceive. As a human being, I know I can't fully understand the depth of His power. He spoke the tallest mountains and deepest oceans into existence. He set the sun, moon, and stars in the sky with a word. How can I begin to comprehend that kind of power? The truth is, I can't. But, when I was fifteen years old, I did get a glimpse of His "immeasurably more" in action.

At thirteen years old, I began to have migraines. I dealt with them for a couple years—the throbbing head, nausea and vomiting, sensitivity to light, and seeing spots in my vision. But when I was fifteen, on top of all those other things, I began experiencing something much scarier.

HOW CAN I BEGIN TO COMPREHEND THAT KIND OF POWER?

During one of my migraines, in addition to not being able to fully see, I found myself not being able to talk or move half of my body. My tongue and left side of my body went completely numb. I felt entirely helpless and trapped. I couldn't even communicate to my mom what was going on. It was the most surreal and horrendous thing I had ever experienced in my short fifteen years of life.

We went to see the neurologist who explained that I had experienced a "complicated migraine," meaning that my blood vessels had constricted so much that it had blocked the flow of oxygen to my brain and other parts of my body. He instructed us to go straight to the ER at the onset of the next migraine, adding his concern that I might have a stroke. That's not the news you want to hear as a teenager.

So, I waited in fear and dread for the next migraine to hit. I usually had one every couple of months, and it always began with what is called the aura—the black spots in my vision. Thankfully, I was at home with my parents when that dreaded day came, and so I quickly told them that a migraine was starting. They began to pack my bags for the hospital, and I climbed into bed and waited to be taken to the ER.

As I lay there, I began to cry like a baby. I was completely overcome with fear. *Was I going to have a stroke? Was I going to make it to the hospital in time? What if I died?* I began to pray and beg God to make it go away. I promised I would follow Him all my life, and I would do whatever He asked me to do if He would just make it stop.

It was then, in between the sobs and pleas, that I heard God's voice unlike I had ever heard it. I distinctly heard the words, "Lacei, sit up." I remember lying there silently, wondering if I had really heard what I thought I had heard. Then, to relieve any doubt, I heard the voice again: "Lacei, sit up."

I slowly sat up in my bed, still unsure of what was going on. But as I sat up, the spots in my vision disappeared. My vision was completely normal again. I looked around the room in confusion, wondering what had just happened. And then, I realized that I had just experienced God's immeasurably more. To this day, I have never again experienced any type of migraine headache. To Him be the glory.

What about you?

Recall a time when you experienced God's "immeasurably more" in your life. Write out what happened.

Take time right now to thank Him for His goodness and power and to give Him the glory He deserves.

Wowed by BEING STILL
by Gail Duford

"Be still and know that I am God! I will be honored by every nation. I will be honored throughout the world." Psalms 46:10 (NLT)

The year was 1993. Our son Paul, a teenager at the time, was so excited to be going with his youth group on a mission trip to Jamaica.

When I first heard about this mission trip and all the fund-raising activities Paul would need to be a part of, I knew he wasn't in a place in his life to participate in raising these funds. As my husband Don and I prayed for our son, the Holy Spirit spoke to me, not in an audible voice, but I knew for certain that I had received a message in regards to Paul going on this mission trip. The Holy Spirit told me to pay for all of the expenses for him to be a part of this trip.

I went to the youth pastor and told him all of this and asked him to let Paul sign up. He agreed to let us pay for his expenses to go to Jamaica. Paul was excited to go experience Jamaican lifestyles. God had definitely led the way for this life lesson for our son.

The first night, Paul called from Jamaica to speak to us, and being a bit home-sick, he exclaimed, "I would run through these streets butt naked to come home!" Oh my! Don and I became more fervent in our prayers that God would not only keep Paul on this trip, but He would also show our son how much he was loved by Him. By the last night in Jamaica, there was a definite change in Paul's counte-nance. He tearfully spoke to us on the phone, telling us about the orphanage and the poor living conditions of the children. He even told us, "I would like to return to Jamaica someday."

The next evening, Don and I were driving to the church around midnight to pick up our precious son. We couldn't wait to hug him and hear about his mission trip. As we approached the corner of two streets, the traffic light was green, and there were very few other cars out at this time of night. Just as we drove into the intersection, a speeding car came from out of nowhere, and it headed directly into the side of our van!

We cried out, "Jesus, help us!" He did. The car just disappeared. Don and I looked in every direction to see where that car should have been, but it simply wasn't there. From **THE CAR JUST DISAPPEARED.** the moment we called out to Jesus, we never saw that car again. We knew that

God had intervened and supernaturally removed that speeding car. If it would have hit us, Don and I probably would have been killed. God spared our lives that night, and we were able to make it to the church to pick up our son.

A verse that I gave to Paul during his teenage years was Psalms 46:10 which begins, "Be still and know that I am God" (NLT). Paul is now a husband, father, and most importantly, a believer in Jesus Christ. He and his wife now own a business that helps people learn how to get jobs. Paul once told me that the experience in the Jamaican orphanage is why he has his business today. Praise God for His direction and His protection. We don't need to worry, only to be still and know. He takes care of the rest.

What about you?

How do you know when the Holy Spirit talks to you?

Is there a situation in your life right now that you find yourself worrying about? Take time to "be still and know" that He is God. Be quiet and allow Him to give you rest and peace.

KNOWING HIS VOICE
by Emily McCarty

"Rejoice always, pray without ceasing, give thanks in all circumstances; for this is the will of God in Christ Jesus for you." 1 Thessalonians 5:16-18 (ESV)

I was hanging out as a friend's house. We were talking, laughing, and drinking coffee. We were having a wonderful conversation about life, God, and family. Our four boys were playing together and getting along nicely.

In the middle of our conversation, the boys started doing what boys do best. They got rowdy. We peeked into the playroom, and they were being quite rambunctious. It was the kind of playing boys do before they start fighting. I was waiting to see if my friend would intervene since it was her house. Instead of leaving them alone or telling them to settle down, she did something I never would have thought to do in that situation.

She said a quick prayer. "God, do I need to intervene?" She paused for a moment, waiting for an answer. "No. Ok." And she went right back to our conversation.

"GOD, DO I NEED TO INTERVENE?"

I thought *this is what it means to pray without ceasing*. This was such a quick moment that I doubt she even remembers it. It seemed to be something she did multiple times a day. But, my mind was blown for a few reasons.

First, she thought to consult God on an everyday situation. How many times a day do I make a split-second decision without first asking the Creator of life? Second, she was able to hear from God so quickly. That line of communication was primed and ready. Third, she knew God's voice well enough to be confident she heard correctly. She was familiar with His voice.

I instantly knew I wanted that type of relationship with God. I had always doubted if I heard correctly and questioned if I even heard from Him at all. I knew then that I needed to get to know the Father's voice and to trust He wouldn't let me mishear Him.

I INSTANTLY KNEW I WANTED THAT TYPE OF RELATIONSHIP WITH GOD.

The conversations I've had with God since that day are astounding to me. He's given me new dreams, new ideas, life changing revelations, and small everyday answers. And you know what? He's never steered me wrong.

What about you?

How do you practically pray without ceasing? What does that look like?

Do you have a relationship with God in which you ask Him even about the "little things" and actually wait for an answer? How does a person develop a relationship like that?

Is the line of communication between you and God "primed and ready"?

The End (Some Final Thoughts)

Now, it's time to circle back around to that "wowed" question: Have you ever been wowed by God? Have you ever been awestruck at His goodness, His power, His holiness, His love?

According to the Cambridge Dictionary, to wow a person is to "make someone feel great excitement or admiration." Does God produce these emotions in you? Honestly, my excitement and admiration for Him has had its highs and lows, not because He has been more or less worthy of it, but because I haven't always taken the time to be still and reflect on how truly amazing He is. Although I had journaled many stories of His goodness and power in my own life, I haven't always paused and reminded myself of them.

As a child, I remember hearing "testimony time" at church. Basically, this involved someone standing up and sharing something the Lord had done in his or her life. I loved hearing those stories because they gave me an extremely powerful gift—HOPE. Although I hadn't yet had the moments with Jesus these stories described, it sparked a thought that maybe these encounters were possible for me too. I remember thinking, *Maybe, just maybe, this Jesus actually does want to show me how real He is and how much He loves me. Maybe someday I can stand up and share stories like that too.*

As a young teenager, I remember still waiting for some of those Jesus encounters and trying to decide if I would continue to wait or move on. I had to choose if this faith in God was going to be mine or just the beliefs of my parents and Sunday school teachers. Doubts flooded my mind as I was surrounded by the messages of my culture and friends at school, and as I battled wanting to live my life my way. Although I still tried to pray, it often felt like my prayers were unheard and unanswered (or at least not answered in a way I preferred). Yet, I still had those nagging memories of other's God-stories, their personal encounters with Jesus I couldn't just dismiss with a teenage "whatever" and an eye-roll.

So, I continued to ask God for my own experiences with Him, my own encounters with His goodness and with His power. He answered my prayer. Sitting alone in my bedroom, I had many precious moments with the Lord, and I discovered that James 4:8 is true. If you come near to God, He really does come near to you. That promise in itself still blows my mind. The God of the Universe pursues a closer relationship with me, actually desires to reveal Himself to ME. Wow. Just wow.

As an adult, I am still seeking to know God more. I am still praying for more and more encounters with Jesus, and He has never disappointed me. Although He doesn't always answer my prayers in my timing or work in the way I think He will (actually He rarely does), He has shown me His power and goodness over and over throughout my life. Now, I have stories of my own to tell, and I feel compelled to "stand up" and continue to share both my own experiences and those of other women in my life.

My prayer is that this book has encouraged you to do the same, that whatever your thoughts are about God, you will seek to know more about Him and about His love for you. I pray you experience your very first or your sixty-fourth encounter with His goodness and power. I pray you feel compelled to "stand up" with me, to share your own stories and bring Him the honor, praise, and glory He deserves. May we never lose our wonder. May we always be wowed by One.

"Great is the LORD! He is most worthy of praise! No one can measure his greatness. Let each generation tell its children of your mighty acts; let them proclaim your power. I will meditate on your majestic, glorious splendor and your wonderful miracles. Your awe-inspiring deeds will be on every tongue; I will proclaim your greatness. Everyone will share the story of your wonderful goodness; they will sing with joy about your righteousness." Psalms 145:3-7 (NLT)

OTHER BOOKS BY KEITH & LACEI GRABILL

Borrowing God's Glasses takes young women beyond a surface knowledge of God and challenges them to actively pursue Him and His Truth. Written in a transparent, down-to-earth style, this book helps readers recognize their God-given identity, discover the extravagant love of their Creator, and boldly live out His vision for their lives. Each chapter is followed by reflection questions, making it perfect for small group study or personal devotions.

It often starts as an innocent attraction, but then pornography becomes a trap many fall into. Although the struggle can be kept a secret for a time, the feelings of powerlessness and entrapment will begin to surface. Is freedom possible? That's what this practical and life-giving book is all about. Whether you are looking for freedom, helping someone who needs it, or just want to continue in freedom, Seven Times is for you. It's time to win. It's time to live free.

UNIQUE DEVOTIONALS FROM
SEARCH FOR THE TRUTH MINISTRIES

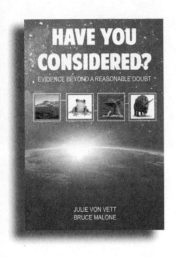

Have You Considered is the third in a series of unique devotionals which present the evidence for creation from every area of science. This 432 page softcover book presents 365 different examples of how well science supports a biblical model for our origins. The book is stunningly illustrated with over 200 full-color illustrations. It is written in a style that is appropriate to be read to young children yet profoundly enjoyable for adults. The book also contains extensive references and includes topical, Bible verse, and subject indexes. It is a phenomenal source for home schoolers, Christian parents, or anyone wanting to know more about nature or creation.

This is the latest of our 365-page daily devotionals giving evidence for the trustworthiness of God's Word from every area of science. God does not want us to simply HOPE He exists, just THINK He exists, or merely BELIEVE He exists. He wants us to KNOW that He exists and KNOW that the Bible is His timeless and changeless revelation to mankind. If you visit the Library of Congress in Washington, D.C., you will notice a stained-glass window saying, "Nature is the art of God." Nature proclaims God's creativity and ingenuity; studying nature confirms God's Word. The more we observe nature and take dominion, the more we find the fingerprints of God. Look within the pages of this book to get just a glimpse. This exquisitely illustrated book is a fascinating expose' on the creativity of God.

See more at www.searchforthetruth.net